Teach·ing Syl·la·ble Pat·terns

Shortcut to Fluency and Comprehension for Striving Adolescent Readers

Lin Carver and Lauren Pantoja

Maupin House by
capstone
professional

Teaching Syllable Patterns:
Shortcut to Fluency and Comprehension for Striving Adolescent Readers
© 2009 Lin Carver and Lauren Pantoja. All Rights Reserved.

Cover design: Studio Montage
Book design and layout: Mickey Cuthbertson

Library of Congress Cataloging-in-Publication Data

Carver, Lin, 1955-
 Teaching syllable patterns : shortcut to fluency and comprehension for striving adolescent readers / Lin Carver and Lauren Pantoja.
     p. cm.
 Includes bibliographical references.
 ISBN 978-1-934338-39-1 (pbk.)
 1. Language arts (Secondary) 2. Grammar, Comparative and general--Syllable--Study and teaching. 3. Reading comprehension. I. Pantoja, Lauren, 1953- II. Title.
 LB1631.C4452 2009
 428.4'0712--dc22
                                        2009011296

Maupin House publishes professional resources for K-12 educators. Contact us for tailored, in-school training or to schedule an author for a workshop or conference. Visit www.maupinhouse.com for free lesson plan downloads.

Maupin House Publishing, Inc. by Capstone Professional
1710 Roe Crest Drive
North Mankato, MN 56003

www.maupinhouse.com

888-262-6135

info@maupinhouse.com

Table of Contents

In·tro·duc·tion

Figuring out why struggling secondary readers can't master the reading process can be a teacher's biggest challenge. Frequently, these students cannot comprehend the meaning of the words they read. But sometimes they just can't read.

Students who fall into the second group can read some sight words, but when they come across a new word they cannot figure it out. They simply don't "get" letter patterns. They haven't internalized the six basic types of English syllables (Rippel, 2008), and without that skill they are unable to decode new words. Their reading is not fluent—it's labored and unsatisfying. Their oral reading performance in class embarrasses them, and to avoid the feeling of failure, they stop participating in class and avoid reading at home (Torgensen, 2004).

Consequently, these students do not have much experience with reading, and their exposure to new vocabulary words, text organization, and academic language is limited (Moats, 2001). Without practice in reading, their comprehension, spelling, and writing skills decline dramatically over time. What may have begun as a fairly simple phonological or word-recognition deficit often becomes a debilitating language and comprehension problem that affects both spoken and written language (National Institute for Literacy, 2007).

Of course, these students should have mastered these basic reading skills a long time ago, so we teachers sometimes forget to check to make sure that they really know *how* to read. Or we may not think it's really our job to teach older students how to read. We hope, unfortunately too often in vain, that they will "get" it at some point on their own. And what secondary teacher has the time or patience to go back and teach those phonemic drills from early reading days?

Drills don't work well with secondary students anyway. But games and activities do. Instead of syllable pattern drills, *Teaching Syllable Patterns* organizes the six basic English syllable patterns into games and activities that can be easily inserted into any teacher's day.

Playing games and doing different activities helps move these skills to the automatic level so that students can pronounce the words they see more quickly. This will enable them to read the passages smoothly and hold onto their meaning. By taking the decoding to an automatic level, students can focus their attention on making meaning from the text.

Students learn the patterns effortlessly and with pleasure. And we have personally seen how quickly the patterns are internalized, providing a true shortcut to improved fluency.

Who Can Use This Book?

Teaching Syllable Patterns is flexible and can be used with intensive reading classes, regular reading classes, or language arts classes at intermediate, middle-school, or high-school levels. Teachers, reading coaches, and tutors can set up the games and activities for whole- or small-group settings to provide intensive work on specific skills, or to tutor one-on-one. It can also be used in home-school settings.

This book lends itself to easily differentiating instruction in any classroom where literacy is the goal. When other students in class are working or reading independently, the games and activities can be used with small groups or individuals who are experiencing difficulty decoding words.

As teachers we modify content and address various learning styles to meet student needs. *Teaching Syllable Patterns* incorporates visual, auditory, and kinesthetic learning modalities. Older students who are still experiencing difficulty in decoding are going to need many opportunities to practice these skills using a variety of methods and learning styles. The easy-to-do games give them that practice.

First Step: Identify the Reading Problem

An informal assessment is the first step in helping your striving students experience success in reading. Listen to your students' oral responses: Do they appear to comprehend meaning when you read to them? Listen to them read: Do they struggle with unknown words? Or do you find that they struggle to read words that are in their spoken vocabulary?

When assessing striving students, it's appropriate to keep a running record or use more formal assessments such as the Woodcock Reading Mastery (Woodcock, 1987) or the Diagnostics Assessment of Reading (Roswell et al, 2005). Group-administered, standardized tests alone will probably not provide enough information, but these tests can be used as a springboard for identifying those students with reading difficulties. Once students are identified as needing reading intervention, use informal assessments to determine the root of the problem.

How to Use This Book

The chapters in *Teaching Syllable Patterns* are intended to be taught in the order they are presented. An organizational chart in Chapter 1 helps illustrate the instructional breakdown of the lessons. The chart indicates the average time for each chapter, but you are, of course, the best judge of how much practice your students need. Different sections can be combined or omitted depending on your students' progress and your classroom-specific needs.

Allow at least a week for each chapter (but you will see that some chapters have two or three weeks' worth of activities). This amount of time gives students enough practice with the newly introduced skills so that each set of skills becomes automatic before you move on to another. The chart in Chapter 1 gives recommended time frames for each lesson or activity.

Each chapter contains weekly "do-nows," which should be used as informal diagnostic tools to help determine which students need additional instruction before the mini-lesson or guided practice with the whole group. The mini-lesson helps students understand the concepts presented in each chapter, and the guided practice enables the students to become proficient with the skills in a supportive environment.

Decoding instruction using these games and activities should not take up an entire lesson. Experience has shown us that students will master the decoding skills more quickly if they are taught in short, ten- to twenty-minute sessions with frequent review.

Because the goal is for students to internalize the patterns—to reach "automaticity"—an activity or game can be repeated as needed. The skills are reinforced through additional independent practice. As the teacher, you are the best judge of how much practice your students need to be successful. Choose the components your students need and skip those that are repetitive.

A post-test covering the skills taught ends each chapter. Nonsense words, also known as "pseudo-words," are incorporated into these post-tests so that you eliminate the factor of sight vocabulary influencing student answers. The post-tests help you determine student progress and guide instruction. You can then decide whether to provide additional practice using the components of the unit or whether the skill has been mastered and students are ready to move on.

For student responses, we recommend the use of individual whiteboards, if at all possible. Students of all ages enjoy using these, and they are a great way to quickly assess students' understanding of skills. Individual whiteboards are inexpensive and can be purchased in large sheets at major hardware stores, which will often cut them into customized, individual squares. Note that when classroom whiteboards are referenced in this book, an interactive whiteboard (such as a SMART™ Board) or overhead projector may be used instead. And, of course, using paper for responses is always an option.

The included CD saves on prep time by providing all of the reproducibles, assessments, and full-color game materials needed for every lesson. Game materials were designed to print clearly in color or black and white, and all game cards include a front and back so that they can be printed two-sided. Just look for the CD icon throughout the book.

Chap·ter 1
How to Teach Syllable Patterns

The following case study of a conversation between one of the authors and a concerned parent illustrates how important it is to accurately diagnose the root of the comprehension problem.

During open house, my student Joey's mom expressed her frustration to me. "Joey's seventh-grade teacher last year said he had a comprehension problem. I don't know how to help him. I made him read all summer, but it doesn't seem to have made a difference."

As an eighth-grade language arts teacher, I know how challenging it can be to help struggling secondary readers master the reading process. I carefully listened to her explain Joey's situation.

"He still is in an extra reading class this year. What am I going to do? He is discouraged and humiliated. The other kids make fun of him. Will this year in your eighth-grade class be any different?"

"I'm glad you brought this to my attention," I responded. "Let me work with Joey in class and see what's happening. Then we can set up a conference to discuss your concerns and come up with a plan to address Joey's needs."

The next day, in an effort to build background knowledge for our literature unit, the class discussed the Arctic Region. I paid special attention to Joey's contributions to the discussion. I noticed that he raised his hand often and had a lot of information to share. He was enthusiastic and engaged. Oral language was clearly one of his strengths. At the end of the period, I asked Joey to sum up our discussion. He was easily able to identify the main idea and some of the supporting details as well.

On Wednesday, I showed a short informational video about the Arctic Region. To end the lesson, I asked students to write three facts, two questions they still had, and one summary statement. This is when I first noticed a problem. Joey really grasped the idea, but his spelling was unbelievably poor. His response was very difficult to read.

Thursday we began the read-aloud from *The Call of the Wild*. All the students were engaged, but I noticed Joey was particularly attentive. During each think-aloud and summarization point, Joey's responses were appropriate. I knew that auditory comprehension was not a problem.

On Friday, as we moved to Chapter Two of our novel, I planned for students to read in pairs. Since we had an odd number of students, I paired with Joey. This gave me an opportunity to hear Joey read without singling him out. Joey was able to read many of the connector words, which were obviously sight words for him. When he came to a multisyllabic word, he could not get any further than the initial phoneme. He stumbled through the first page, hesitating often, asking for assistance, and substituting incorrect words. Reading was definitely a struggle for him.

I had the information I needed. When I spoke to his mother the following week, I was excited to share what I had observed. "Joey has very strong auditory processing skills and good language development," I began. "He is able to summarize and identify important details and makes accurate inferences and predictions. These are all skills that will help him succeed in mastering the reading process."

His mother looked surprised and a little puzzled. "But they told me he has a comprehension problem!" she said.

"Yes, he has a comprehension problem; he can't understand what he is reading. However, his lack of understanding is because he cannot identify many words. Consequently, he is missing so many words in the text that it doesn't make sense. This is actually good news, though, because this type of difficulty can be corrected."

I continued, "I should add that his poor spelling is an indicator that he also has some difficulty with visual memory. My plan is to provide him with a means of figuring out words that is not totally dependent on visual memory. I can tell that Joey has had some phonics instruction in the past because he recognizes the initial sounds in words, but he doesn't seem to understand how to figure out longer words. This is a great class for Joey to be in because some of the other students in this class are experiencing similar difficulties.

"Because he is an older student, much of what he is expected to read includes longer words. Joey needs a way to chunk these words into smaller parts, but he doesn't know how. I'm going to help him divide and conquer English words so he will be able to read new words," I told her.

I explained that English words are composed of six different types of syllable patterns which can be combined to form longer words. A syllable is determined by the vowel sound and the consonant sounds that surround that vowel. Vowels can make long, short, or diphthong sounds depending on their place in the syllable.

I then explained my plan in more detail to Joey's mother. "To help Joey, we will take one type of syllable at a time. That way Joey and other students experiencing the same difficulty will become proficient with one pattern before another is introduced. Because they tend to be confusing to students, we have also included the soft and hard sounds for "c" and "g" and the various spellings for the /sh/ sound. The great thing about this approach is that, since students have a basic understanding of phonics, they can quickly build to reading the longer multisyllabic grade-level words."

One syllable at a time: That is the approach I took with Joey in my eighth-grade language arts class, and it's an approach that works for striving readers in a variety of settings. When you add the dimension of teaching the syllable types in games and activities, the approach works to create fluent readers who automatically see and apply the basic syllable rules.

Building Background Knowledge

A syllable is a combination of letters with only one vowel sound. In English there are six basic types of syllables: CVC, CV, Cle, R-control, CVCe, and CVVC (Wilson, 1996). When combined, these types of syllables form longer words. The placement of the vowel is what determines the type of syllable.

In the names of the syllable types, "C" refers to the consonants. It could refer to one consonant or a consonant blend or diphthong. "V" refers to the vowels. There can only be one vowel sound in each syllable. Vowels open the mouth and allow us to blend the sounds in each syllable. The small "e" refers to a syllable that ends with that letter. The R-control syllable has an "r" immediately following the vowel.

Teaching the Syllables

You, the teacher, begin your syllable instruction by teaching the common CVC syllable, typically thought of as the "short vowel" syllable. These syllables are found in short words and can be combined to form longer words. For example, the word "cat" is a CVC but so are "clap," "bent," and "in." The important factor is not how many consonants there are, but that there is at least one consonant after the vowel to close the syllable so that the vowel makes a short sound. Those CVC syllables can then be combined to form longer words like "napkin" and "contempt." By the end of the first week's practice, you will notice that students are already becoming successful with grade-level words.

After about two weeks, you will introduce the CV syllable in which the vowel appears at the end, such as in words like "be" and "go." The CV syllable can be combined with the CVC syllable to form words like "tulip" and "pupil."

It's at this point that explicit instruction begins to set up the games and activities that help students combine the different types of syllables. When a student comes to a word he doesn't know, ask him to first count the number of vowel sounds. If there are two separate vowel sounds, the word has two syllables.

A student can underline the vowels, then count the number of consonants between the vowel sounds. If there are two consonants between the vowel sounds, the word gets divided between the consonants because the word is composed of two CVC syllables. The word "mitten" is an example of this. If there is one consonant between the vowel sounds, the word is typically divided before the consonant, so the first syllable becomes a CV syllable, as in the word "tulip."

The goal in decoding is to get the unknown word into a word that makes sense and is in the student's vocabulary (Bhattarya & Ehri, 2004). If dividing before the consonant does not produce a word that sounds logical in the sentence, the student needs to divide after the consonant and see if that produces a word that makes sense. The two pronunciations of "present" are an example of this rule.

The goal is to get this process to an automatic level. It takes some practice, but practicing this skill in ten- to twenty-minute intervals makes it more manageable, so plan to spend three weeks on just the first two types of syllables.

Once students are proficient with the CVC and the CV syllables, the Cle syllable is introduced. This is an easy syllable because it can only be used as a final syllable in a word. The vowel makes neither a long nor a short sound, but rather a totally different sound like in the word "bubble." In the Cle syllable the "le" always takes the consonant before it. The word "title" is divided as "ti-tle" because the "le" keeps the "t." The first syllable is a CV syllable. This also explains why "wiggle" must have two "g's" in the center. The first "g" keeps the first vowel short. "Wig" is a CVC syllable.

After about five weeks, you can begin working on the R-control syllable. This is another easy one. What is nice about the R-control syllable is that there are really only three different sounds that the vowel can make. The R-control syllable has an "r" immediately following the vowel, like in the word "car" or "firm." There is the /ar/ sound, the /er/ sound, and the /or/ sound. Readers only have to learn three different sounds. The combinations /er/, /ir/, and /ur/ all make the same sound.

During the sixth week, the CVCe syllable is introduced. Since students are familiar with the long vowel sound, this syllable will also be easy. This combination can only be used as a final syllable in a word. The "e" at the end of the syllable is silent and causes the vowel before it to make the long sound, as in the word bike.

After students understand the types of syllables that can be used at the end of words, they are ready to develop an understanding of the rules for adding suffixes. The type of final syllable in the root word will determine how the suffix is added to the root word. The initial grapheme of the suffix will also affect how the two are combined. For example, "hope" drops the final "e" before a suffix beginning with a vowel but not before a suffix beginning with a consonant. "Hope" can become "hoping" and "hopeful." The final consonant of a CVC syllable doubles before a suffix beginning with a vowel but not one beginning with a consonant. For example, "cat" becomes "catty" and "catlike." Starting the eighth week, you will look at the relationship between the suffix and the root word. Different suffixes can change the appearance of the root word.

Around the ninth week of school, you will start on the last type of syllable, the CVVC. This is the most difficult syllable type and will take a few weeks to master. On the most basic level, the first vowel makes the long sound and the second one is silent, like in the word "boat." When you teach this syllable, students also learn about the single vowel sounds in diphthongs such as /ou/, /ow/, /au/, /aw/, /oi/, and /oy/.

During the twelfth, thirteenth, and fourteenth weeks, you will look at two additional, more difficult areas: the hard and soft "c" and "g" and additional spellings for the /sh/ sounds.

Four months is all you need to help striving students divide and conquer new words with the help of syllable pattern knowledge. In that time, they will have developed the skills they need to be successful in the reading process. A more detailed breakdown of the lessons, activities, and timeframes in this book is presented in the Scope and Sequence chart on the following pages.

Scope & Sequence

Sequence	Suggested Time Frame	Moving to Automaticity	Time	Materials
Week 1: CVC	Day 1	Do-now	10 min.	CVC syllable prompts
	Day 1	Mini-lesson	20 min.	Example multisyllabic words, nonsense word list, pictures for short vowel sounds, letter cubes or lap-sized white boards
	Day 2	Do-now	10 min.	Nonsense word prompts
	Day 2	Mini-lesson from Day 1 cont'd.	20 min.	Example multisyllabic words, nonsense word list, pictures for short vowel sounds, letter cubes or lap-sized white boards
	Day 3	Do-now	10 min.	Syllable combination prompts
	Day 3	Guided Practice	20 min.	Syllable chart, letter cubes, or lap-sized white boards
	Day 3 or 4	Game—Bingo	20 min.	Bingo cards, pieces to cover space on cards, blank 3" x 5" cards, CVC syllable cards
	Day 3 or 4	Extension	10 min.	CVC syllable cards
	Day 4	Do-now	10 min.	
	Day 4	Independent Practice	15 min.	Short vowel review worksheet
	Day 5	Do-now	10 min.	
	Day 5	Post-test	20 min.	Post-test—CVC
Week 2: CV	Day 1	Do-now	10 min.	
	Day 1	Mini-lesson	15 min.	CV syllable chart, white board, dry erase markers
	Day 2	Do-now	10 min.	Syllable matching list
	Day 2	Guided Practice	15 min.	CV two-syllable word chart, white board, dry erase markers
	Day 2 or 3	Game—Reaching the Pot of Gold	10 min.	Pot of Gold game board, Pot of Gold syllable cards, die, game markers
	Day 3	Do-now	10 min.	Open-syllable word search
	Day 3 or 4	Independent Practice	10 min.	Open-syllable crossword puzzle
	Day 4	Do-now	10 min.	Two-syllable word prompts
	Day 4	Extension	10 min.	CV/CVC syllable word cards
	Day 5	Do-now	10 min.	Three-syllable word prompts
	Day 5	Post-test	20 min.	Post-test—CV

Sequence	Suggested Time Frame	Moving to Automaticity	Time	Materials
Week 3: CVC/CV	Day 1	Do-now	10 min.	Syllable matching list
	Day 1	Mini-lesson	10 min.	Syllable sort graphic organizer, syllable sort cards, class white board
	Day 2	Do-now	10 min.	Syllable fill-in-the-blanks
	Day 2	Mini-lesson from Day 1 cont'd.	10 min.	Syllable sort graphic organizer, syllable sort cards, class white board
	Day 3	Do-now	10 min.	CV syllable prompts
	Day 3	Guided Practice	15 min.	White boards and dry erase markers, lists A and B
	Day 4	Do-now	10 min.	Medial syllables prompts
	Day 4	Game—Syllable Memory	10 min.	Syllable memory cards
	Day 4	Independent Practice	10 min.	CV/CVC worksheet
	Day 5	Do-now	10 min.	Nonsense word prompts
	Day 5	Post-test	20 min.	Post-test—CV/CVC
Week 4: Cle syllable	Day 1	Do-now	10 min.	
	Day 1	Mini-lesson	15 min.	Cle syllable graphic organizer, Cle syllable sort cards
	Day 2	Do-now	10 min.	ABC sort
	Day 2	Guided practice	20 min.	Individual white boards, dry erase markers, Cle word chart
	Day 3	Do-now	10 min.	Cle fill-in-the-blanks
	Day 3 or 4	Extension	15 min.	Baseball memory cards, classroom baseball diamond
	Day 4	Do-now	10 min.	
	Day 4	Independent practice	15 min.	Syllable chart, small blank cards
	Day 4	Game—Baseball	20 min.	Baseball memory cards, classroom baseball diamond
	Day 5	Do-now	10 min.	Cle word search
	Day 5	Post-test	20 min.	Post-test—Cle

Sequence	Suggested Time Frame	Moving to Automaticity	Time	Materials
Week 5: R-control	Day 1	Do-now	10 min.	
	Day 1	Mini-lesson	20 min.	R-control vowel combination cards, R-control vowel word chart, white boards, dry erase markers
	Day 2	Do-now	10 min.	R-control combination prompts #1
	Day 2	Mini-lesson from Day 1 cont'd.	20 min.	R-control vowel combination cards, R-control vowel word chart, white boards, dry erase markers
	Day 3	Do-now	10 min.	R-control combination prompts #2
	Day 3	Guided Practice	15 min.	Vocabulary graphic organizer, "Sportsmanship" story
	Day 3	Game—Pyramid Game	15 min.	Pyramid, timer
	Day 4	Do-now	10 min.	R-control fill-in-the-blanks
	Day 4	Independent Practice	15 min.	R-control vowel worksheet #1
	Day 4	Extension	15 min.	R-control vowel worksheet #2
	Day 5	Do-now	10 min.	Syllable matching list
	Day 5	Post-test	20 min.	Post-test—R-control syllables
Week 6: CVCe	Day 1	Do-now	10 min.	CVCe vocabulary fill-in-the-blanks #1
	Day 1	Mini-lesson	10 min.	Classroom white board, example words
	Day 2	Do-now	10 min.	CVCe vocabulary fill-in-the-blanks #2
	Day 2	Guided Practice	15 min.	Classroom white board, notebook paper
	Day 3	Do-now	10 min.	CVCe vocabulary fill-in-the-blanks #3
	Day 3	Game—Rolling Along	15 min.	Rolling Along word cards
	Day 4	Do-now	10 min.	CVCe vocabulary fill-in-the-blanks #4
	Day 4	Game—Rolling Along	15 min.	Rolling Along word cards
	Day 5	Do-now	10 min.	CVCe vocabulary fill-in-the-blanks #5
	Day 5	Independent Practice	15 min.	Cloze extension worksheet #1

Sequence	Suggested Time Frame	Moving to Automaticity	Time	Materials
Week 7: Two-syllable CVCe	Day 1	Do-now	10 min.	CVCe vocabulary fill-in-the-blanks #6
	Day 1	Mini-lesson	15 min.	Classroom white boards
	Day 2	Do-now	10 min.	CVCe vocabulary fill-in-the-blanks #7
	Day 2	Guided Practice	15 min.	Blend graphic organizer, digraph graphic organizer, CVCe word list
	Day 2 or 3	Game—Star-spangled Path	15 min.	Star-spangled cards, Star-spangled game board, dice
	Day 3	Do-now	10 min.	CVCe vocabulary fill-in-the-blanks #8
	Day 3	Independent Practice	15 min.	Cloze extension worksheet #2
	Day 4	Do-now	10 min.	CVCe vocabulary fill-in-the-blanks #9
	Day 4	Extension	15 min.	Multisyllabic CVCe word list
	Day 5	Do-now	10 min.	CVCe vocabulary fill-in-the-blanks #10
	Day 5	Post-test	20 min.	Post-test—CVCe
Week 8: Adding suffixes	Day 1	Do-now	10 min.	Suffix fill-in-the-blanks #1
	Day 1	Mini-lesson	15 min.	Suffix cards #1, two-way suffix graphic organizer
	Day 2	Do-now	10 min.	Suffix fill-in-the-blanks #2
	Day 2	Mini-lesson from Day 1 cont'd.	15 min.	Suffix cards #1, two-way suffix graphic organizer
	Day 3	Do-now	10 min.	Root/suffix match #1
	Day 3	Guided Practice	15 min.	Category cards, suffix cards #2, four blank index cards per pair of students
	Day 3 or 4	Game—Ing	15 min.	"Ing" cards
	Day 4	Do-now	10 min.	Root/suffix match #2
	Day 4	Independent Practice	15 min.	Suffix worksheet
	Day 5	Do-now	10 min.	Root/suffix chart
	Day 5	Post-test	20 min.	Post-test—Suffixes

Sequence	Suggested Time Frame	Moving to Automaticity	Time	Materials
Week 9: CVVC— digraphs	Day 1	Do-now	10 min.	Vowel combination prompts
	Day 1	Mini-lesson	15 min.	Vowel team words
	Day 2	Do-now	10 min.	Homonym practice
	Day 2	Guided Practice	15 min.	Whiteboards, single- and multiple-syllable vowel digraph cards
	Day 3	Do-now	10 min.	Vowel combination word scramble
	Day 3	Guided Practice from Day 2 cont'd.	15 min.	Whiteboards, single- and multiple-syllable vowel digraph cards
	Day 4	Do-now	10 min.	CVVC rhyme
	Day 4	Game—Winning Teams	20 min.	Vowel team cards, classroom white board
	Day 5	Do-now	10 min.	
	Day 5	Extension	20 min.	Vowel team cards, class white board
	Day 5	Independent Practice	20 min.	Vowel team worksheet
Week 10: CVVC— oi/oy, ou/ow	Day 1	Do-now	10 min.	Diphthong fill-in-the-blanks #1
	Day 1	Mini-lesson	15 min.	Paper and pencil
	Day 2	Do-now	10 min.	Syllable matching #1
	Day 2	Guided Practice	15 min.	Diphthong cards, word sort graphic organizer, word sort list, white boards, dry erase markers
	Day 3	Do-now	10 min.	Diphthong fill-in-the-blanks #2
	Day 3	Guided Practice from Day 2 cont'd.	15 min.	Diphthong cards, word sort graphic organizer, word sort list, white boards, dry erase markers
	Day 4	Do-now	10 min.	Syllable matching #2
	Day 4	Game—Racing Fever	20 min.	Die, place holders for the game, Racing Fever word cards, Racing Fever game board
	Day 4 or 5	Extension	20 min.	Die, place holders for the game, Racing Fever game board, Racing Fever word cards
	Day 5	Do-now	10 min.	Diphthong fill-in-the-blanks #3
	Day 5	Independent Practice	20 min.	Diphthong worksheet

Sequence	Suggested Time Frame	Moving to Automaticity	Time	Materials
Week 11: CVVC— au/aw	Day 1	Do-now	10 min.	Diphthong fill-in-the-blanks #4
	Day 1	Mini-lesson	20 min.	Classroom white board, example "au/aw" words
	Day 2	Do-now	10 min.	Syllable prompts
	Day 2	Guided Practice	20 min.	Set of "au/aw" cards for each student
	Day 3	Do-now	10 min.	Syllable matching #3
	Day 3	Game—"AU/ AW" Password	20 min.	One checkbook cover for each player; Password set A, set B, and help cards for each team
	Day 4	Do-now	10 min.	Syllable matching #4
	Day 4	Independent Practice	20 min.	"aw/au" word search
	Day 5	Do-now	10 min.	Syllable count
	Day 5	Post-test	20 min.	Post-test—CVVC
Week 12: Soft and hard "c"	Day 1	Do-now	10 min.	Soft "c" passage
	Day 1	Mini-lesson	15 min.	"C" word sort graphic organizer #1, "C" word cards #1
	Day 2	Do-now	10 min.	Hard "c" passage
	Day 2	Guided Practice	15 min.	"C" word cards #2, "C" word sort graphic organizer #2
	Day 3	Do-now	10 min.	
	Day 3	Game—Checkers	20 min.	Checkers word board, Checkers pieces
	Day 4	Do-now	10 min.	"C" nonsense words
	Day 4	Extension	15 min.	Checkers word board, Checkers pieces
	Day 5	Do-now	10 min.	
	Day 5	Independent Practice	15 min.	"C" worksheet

Sequence	Suggested Time Frame	Moving to Automaticity	Time	Materials
Week 13: Soft and hard "g"	Day 1	Do-now	10 min.	Soft "g" passage
	Day 1	Mini-lesson	15 min.	"G" word cards #1, "G" word sort graphic organizer #1
	Day 2	Do-now	10 min.	Hard "g" passage
	Day 2	Guided Practice	15 min.	"G" word sort graphic organizer #2, "G" word cards #2
	Day 3	Do-now	10 min.	
	Day 3	Game—The Boss	15 min.	The Boss game board, The Boss cards, playing pieces, die
	Day 4	Do-now	10 min.	"G" nonsense words
	Day 4	Independent Practice	15 min.	"G" worksheet
	Day 5	Do-now	10 min.	
	Day 5	Post-test	20 min.	Post-test—Soft and hard "c" and "g"
Week 14: Additional sounds for /sh/	Day 1	Do-now	10 min.	/Sh/ passage #1
	Day 1	Mini-lesson	15 min.	Classroom board
	Day 2	Do-now	10 min.	Root word prompts #1
	Day 2	Guided Practice	15 min.	/Sh/ word cards, tape, lap-size white boards
	Day 3	Do-now	10 min.	Root word prompts #2
	Day 3	Game—Hitting the Mark	15 min.	Target, Target word cards, sticky ball
	Day 4	Do-now	10 min.	Root word prompts #3
	Day 4	Independent Practice	15 min.	Newspaper articles, highlighters
	Day 5	Do-now	10 min.	Root word prompts #4
	Day 5	Post-test	20 min.	Post-test—/Sh/
Week 15: Final assessment	Day 1	Game—Final Bingo: Syllable Identification	20 min.	Final Bingo game board and word cards, playing pieces to cover spaces on cards, blank Bingo card
	Day 2	Game—Final Bingo: Syllable Identification from Day 1 cont'd.	20 min.	Final Bingo game board and word cards, playing pieces to cover spaces on cards, blank Bingo card
	Day 3	Game—Graduation	20 min.	Graduation game board and cards, playing pieces, die
	Day 4	Game—Graduation from Day 3 cont'd.	20 min.	Graduation game board and cards, playing pieces, die
	Days 1–5: Individual Assessments	Running Records	10 min.	Final assessment passage—student copy, Assessment matrix

Chap·ter 2
CVC Syllable

Sequence	Suggested Time Frame	Moving to Automaticity	Time	Materials
Week 1: CVC	Day 1	Do-now	10 min.	CVC syllable prompts
	Day 1	Mini-lesson	20 min.	Example multisyllabic words, nonsense word list, pictures for short vowel sounds, letter cubes or lap-sized white boards
	Day 2	Do-now	10 min.	Nonsense word prompts
	Day 2	Mini-lesson from Day 1 cont'd.	20 min.	Example multisyllabic words, nonsense word list, pictures for short vowel sounds, letter cubes or lap-sized white boards
	Day 3	Do-now	10 min.	Syllable combination prompts
	Day 3	Guided Practice	20 min.	Syllable chart, letter cubes, or lap-sized white boards
	Day 3 or 4	Game—Bingo	20 min.	Bingo cards, pieces to cover space on cards, blank 3" x 5" cards, CVC syllable cards
	Day 3 or 4	Extension	10 min.	CVC syllable cards
	Day 4	Do-now	10 min.	
	Day 4	Independent Practice	15 min.	Short vowel review worksheet
	Day 5	Do-now	10 min.	
	Day 5	Post-test	20 min.	Post-test—CVC

Week 1

Day 1

Do-now
Chapter 2:
CVC syllable prompts

CVC syllable prompts

Write the word and indicate whether it is a CVC syllable.

Prompts	Answers
1. thrust	yes
2. imp	yes (Note: Remember that in the CVC syllable, the first C is optional.)
3. coast	no
4. drive	no
5. crash	yes

Mini-lesson
Chapter 2:
Nonsense word list

Note: You can do this exercise on both Days 1 and 2.
- **Time:** Twenty minutes on two different days.
- **Goal:** To develop an understanding of syllables in general and the CVC syllable specifically.
- **Materials:** Example multisyllabic words, nonsense word list, pictures for short vowel sounds, letter cubes or lap-sized white boards.
- **Overview:** While listening to or looking at words, students will identify the number of syllables in the word. Students will also identify the short vowel sound in a CVC syllable.

Directions

Students who have difficulty reading often do not understand how to determine the sounds letters make in longer words. They generally have learned the sounds for the individual phonemes, but don't know how to combine these phonemes into meaningful units. So when they encounter a word that is not in their sight vocabulary, they are unsure how to determine which of the sounds the letters or graphemes make in the word. They usually have learned the long and short vowel sounds but are unsure when to use each sound. Because the position of a letter in a syllable determines what sound that letter will make, English can be frustrating. Students need to understand how the position of letters in the syllable impacts their pronunciation.

The first concept that students need to master is the concept of a syllable. In English there are six basic types of syllables. Each syllable can have only one vowel sound. Students can orally identify syllables by clapping or counting the number of times their chin drops when they say the word. Begin by dictating the words on the following page and have the students identify the number of syllables in each word. The students should indicate the number of syllables in each word by writing the information on white boards or by holding up that number of fingers.

gigantic
memorize
contemplate
scrutinize
flank
producer

Students usually don't have difficulty identifying the number of syllables in a word they hear. However, this concept is a little more difficult when students are asked to *read* an unknown word. The easiest way to teach this concept to older students is through the use of nonsense words, so that the actual decoding skill is being taught instead of students simply recognizing the word by sight. The use of nonsense words directly addresses the sounds made as a result of specific letter combinations.

Have the students work in pairs to determine the number of syllables in each of these nonsense words. Remind students that the vowels are "a," "e," "i," "o," "u," and sometimes "y." You may need to review with students that "y" can be used as a vowel, and that it can make a long /i/ sound or a long /e/ sound at the end of a syllable, or a short /i/ sound in the middle of a syllable. The letter "y" will be covered more extensively in the CV chapter.

Students should underline each vowel or vowel combination to determine the number of syllables. When two vowels are next to each other, they typically make one sound. The letter "e" at the end of the word is usually silent and does not make a new syllable.

Nonsense word list: How many syllables?

glastic	consymtrat
flinster	cainstar
greennaper	stilleppy
insulationly	stecreat
bersonape	abconstrate

Answers

glastic	2	consymtrat	3
flinster	2	cainstar	2
greennaper	3	stilleppy	3
insulationly	5	stecreat	2
bersonape	3	abconstrate	3

Now that students understand the concept of a syllable, they are ready to start working with the CVC syllable. This type of syllable can easily be combined with other syllables to form longer words. Give each pair of students a set of Scrabble letters or magnetic letters that they can use to master this concept. Remind students that they were probably exposed to the short vowels in the primary grades, but they may have forgotten the sounds that these vowels make. It may be necessary to review the short vowel sounds. You'll begin by identifying a picture to associate with each short vowel sound, since it's easier to remember a picture than an isolated phoneme.

When a word-picture is chosen, make sure that the sound of the vowel is clear. Choose a word-picture where the vowel sound is at the beginning of the word, since it is easier for students to identify the vowel sound at the beginning of the word rather than in the middle. Possible word-pictures that can be used for each vowel sound are identified below.

A=apple
E=egg
I=igloo
O=octopus
U=umbrella

Use the same word-pictures each time you work on the short vowel sound, so that the picture is linked to the vowel sound in students' minds.

The CVC or closed syllable has one short vowel sound. Explain that a closed syllable has at least one consonant immediately following the vowel. It may begin with a consonant or a consonant blend, or it may begin directly with the vowel. "In," "pen," "sect," and "thrush" are all closed or CVC syllables and have a short vowel sound. These could be single-syllable words or syllables of multisyllabic words. Once students can recognize closed syllables, they are ready to begin writing them as well. Within the lessons of this book, encoding (writing) and decoding (reading) are taught simultaneously.

Day 2

Do-now

Chapter 2:
Nonsense word prompts

Nonsense word prompts

Underline each vowel sound and determine how many syllables are in each nonsense word.

Prompts		Answers
1.	inbert	2
2.	gymnattum	3
3.	conflictant	3
4.	thrump	1
5.	anthronnic	3

Mini-lesson

Continue from Day 1.

Day 3

Do-now

Chapter 2:
Syllable combination prompts

Syllable combination prompts

Combine a syllable in the first column with a syllable in the second column to form a two-syllable word.

Column 1	Column 2	Answers
in	ic	invest
con	chen	contempt
muf	vest	muffin
kit	fin	kitchen
tox	tempt	toxic

Guided Practice

Chapter 2:
Syllable chart

- **Time:** Twenty minutes on one day.
- **Goal:** To practice combining CVC syllables to form multisyllabic words.
- **Materials:** Syllable chart, letter cubes, or lap-sized white boards.
- **Overview:** Students will combine syllables to form words.

Directions

The following chart of nonsense "words" is actually a list of syllables that can be combined to form multisyllabic words. This practice will allow students to quickly move to decoding longer words. As students understand that they are able to decode longer words, and not just "baby" words, they will be more motivated to apply newly developing decoding skills regularly. These decoding skills, which can be transferred immediately to any content area, will quickly increase the number of words students can read, and their reading vocabulary will not be limited to the words they have memorized from direct instruction.

Dictate syllables and have students work in pairs to practice encoding, or writing, them. Listed below are some examples of closed syllables that can be used to provide practice in decoding closed syllables, identifying short vowel sounds, or encoding closed syllables. They can also be used with the Bingo game that follows.

Syllable chart

vent	sub	mit	muf	vest	stub
sub	fin	vest	stub	tact	in
flict	bas	an	gel	plan	et
con	tent	at	tempt	com	mand
ket	flat	ten	tox	ic	bas
trich	amp	tract	rest	cas	ket
nos	tril	at	tack	bon	net
ten	dent	cab	in	sect	con
cept	ras	cal	vent	hob	bit
rab	bit	ex	cel	spect	ab
stract	os	vent	sub	ject	roc
ket	pan	el	ham	mock	thrush

Game—Bingo

Chapter 2:
Blank Bingo card

Note: You can do this exercise on either Day 3 or Day 4.

- **Time:** Twenty minutes on one day.
- **Goal:** To develop an understanding of the CVC syllables and how they can be combined to form words.
- **Materials:** Bingo cards, pieces to cover space on cards, blank 3" x 5" cards, CVC syllable cards.
- **Overview:** Groups of two to twenty students will identify short vowel sounds in CVC syllables. The first student to cover a complete row is the winner.
- **Objective:** To be the first student to cover a complete row or column on the board.

Directions

1. Give each player a blank Bingo card and a set of blank 3" x 5" cards.
2. Each player creates her individual Bingo card by writing one vowel in each square.
3. To fill the board, each vowel will need to be written in five different squares. For example, there will be five randomly placed "a's," five randomly placed "e's," and five randomly placed "i's," "o's," and "u's." Because students choose the placement of their vowels on the card, each Bingo card will be unique.
4. Shuffle the syllable cards and place in one pile.
5. The teacher reads the first syllable card.
6. Each player covers one space that corresponds with the vowel sound in the word.
7. Each player also writes the syllable on a blank index card.
8. The player who covers five squares in a row first wins the Bingo game if he is able to read back from his index cards the syllables that have been called.
9. If that player is unable to read all the index cards correctly, play continues until another player calls Bingo and reads all the index cards correctly.
10. The student who wins the Bingo game uses the teacher's cards to be the caller for the next game.

Sample completed Bingo card

A	E	I	A	O
E	I	U	I	E
O	O	I	U	A
U	A	E	A	O
I	E	O	U	I

Extension

Note: You can do this exercise on either Day 3 or Day 4.
- **Time:** Ten minutes on one day.
- **Goal:** To combine CVC syllables to form multisyllabic words.
- **Materials:** CVC syllable cards.
- **Overview:** Teams of two to twenty students will combine CVC syllables to form multisyllabic words.

Directions

After the game, students work with a partner to try to combine the syllables they wrote on their index cards to form two-syllable words. The pair of students who forms the most two-syllable words in a specified amount of time is declared the winner.

Day 4

Do-now

Choose a name that is significant to your students and ask them to compose as many CVC words from the name as possible. Set a five-minute time limit and at the end of the limit compare the lists.

Example: University of Florida

fin	fad	sir	sit
yen	lid	fun	ton
tin			

Answers will vary.

Independent Practice 💿 Chapter 2: Short vowel review workseet
- **Time:** Fifteen minutes on one day.
- **Goal:** To practice working with CVC syllables.
- **Materials:** Short vowel review worksheet.
- **Overview:** Working independently, students will complete the worksheet.

Directions

The following reproducible worksheet is provided to reinforce students' abilities in identifying syllables and in combining syllables to form multisyllabic words.

Short vowel review worksheet

In the first section, underline the vowels and determine how many syllables are in the nonsense words and then write the number of syllables after the word.

respintet   chompelling   grespect

abdominem   stimpellet   pallent

schultz   monninep   glendrimpt

Using the syllables in the word bank, combine them to form real two or three syllable words. Write the words on the lines below. A syllable can be used more than once.

muf	bas	cab	man	rip	in
con	in	ic	bas	un	stan
fin	vex	ket	tal	rob	den
ped	tend	con	tent	der	dard
set	tel	graph	spect	con	vict
ab	chap	stract	el	com	ment

_____

_____

_____

_____

_____

_____

_____

_____

_____

_____

_____

Answers

In the first section underline the vowels and determine how many syllables are in the nonsense words and then write the number of syllables after the word.

respintet: 3   chompelling: 3   grespect: 2

abdominem: 4   stimpellet: 3   pallent: 2

schultz: 1   monninep: 3   glendrimpt: 2

Using the syllables in the word bank below, combine them to form real two- or three-syllable words. Write the words on the lines below. A syllable can be used more than once.

muf	bas	cab	man	rip	in
con	in	ic	bas	un	stan
fin	vex	ket	tal	rob	den
ped	tend	con	tent	set	plex
set	tel	graph	spect	con	vict
ab	chap	stract	el	com	ment

Possible Answers

| comment | chapel | inspect | convex | convict | basket | robin |
| muffin | abstract | mantel | subset | content | complex | graphic |

Day 5

Do-now

Give students a word (for example, "much"). Set the timer for one minute. Students must create a chain of words that begin with the final consonant sound of each previous word in the CVC pattern. After one minute, students stop and share their words with a partner.

Example: chin, nun, nod, dish, shod, dim, mush, sham.

Indicate how many syllables are in each word. If the word can be divided into syllables, indicate how it is divided.

Example: trispen   _2 tris * pen_

1. strantummet   _____
2. cranst   _____
3. thrambim   _____
4. drinnic   _____
5. nymmun   _____
6. plentem   _____
7. quist   _____
8. unbinnem   _____
9. antomvun   _____
10. yitpamruc   _____

Write the words that your teacher dictates for each question.

1. _____
2. _____
3. _____
4. _____
5. _____

6. _____
7. _____
8. _____
9. _____
10. _____

Read the following passage orally.

The Contep and the Fristic

A contep was awakened from a strippet by a fristic running over his radbim. Getting up amgastly, he inhabbitted him and was about to kill him, when the fristic detted, saying: "If you would only imcrast my temp, I would be sure to ventum your inrotness." The contep laughed and let him go.

It happened shortly after this that the contep was caught by some huntrepts, who bound him by ropes to the ground. The fristic notted his roar, and came to smand the rope with his treth, and set him grib. He protted, "You thranded the mespast of my ever being able to help you. I now know that it is possibbet for even a fristic to benefit from a contep."

Answers

1. strantummet — <u>3</u> stran * tum * met
2. cranst — <u>1</u>
3. thrambim — <u>2</u> thram * bim
4. drinnic — <u>2</u> drin * nic
5. nybmun — <u>2</u> nyb * mun
6. plentem — <u>2</u> plen * tem
7. quist — <u>1</u>
8. unbinnem — <u>3</u> un * bin * nem
9. antomvun — <u>3</u> an * tom * vun
10. yitpamruc — <u>3</u> yit * pam * ruc

1. frand
2. contrist
3. brith
4. clost
5. yundat
6. slemp
7. trunt
8. grantic
9. sistan
10. flost

The <u>Con * tep</u> and the <u>Fris * tic</u>

A <u>con * teb</u> was awakened from a <u>strip * pet</u> by a <u>fris * tic</u> <u>run * ning</u> over his <u>rad * bim</u>. Getting up <u>am * gast * ly</u>, he <u>in * hab * bit * ted</u> him and was about to kill him, when the <u>fris * tic</u> <u>det *</u> <u>ted</u>, saying: "If you would only <u>im * crast</u> my <u>temp</u>, I would be sure to <u>ven * tum</u> your <u>in * rot *</u> <u>ness</u>." The <u>con * tep</u> laughed and let him go.

It <u>hap * pened</u> shortly after this that the <u>con * tep</u> was caught by some <u>hun * trepts</u>, who bound him by ropes to the ground. The <u>fris * tic</u> <u>not * ted</u> his roar, and came to <u>smand</u> the rope with his <u>treth</u>, and set him <u>grib</u>. He <u>prot * ted</u>, "You <u>thran * ded</u> the <u>mes * past</u> of my ever being able to help you. I now know that it is <u>pos * sib * bet</u> for even a <u>fris * tic</u> to benefit from a <u>con *</u> <u>tep</u>."

Scoring: Number of underlined words correct   /30

Chap·ter 3
CV Syllable

Sequence	Suggested Time Frame	Moving to Automaticity	Time	Materials
Week 2: CV	Day 1	Do-now	10 min.	
	Day 1	Mini-lesson	15 min.	CV syllable chart, white board, dry erase markers
	Day 2	Do-now	10 min.	Syllable matching list
	Day 2	Guided Practice	15 min.	CV two-syllable word chart, white board, dry erase markers
	Day 2 or 3	Game—Reaching the Pot of Gold	10 min.	Pot of Gold game board, Pot of Gold syllable cards, die, game markers
	Day 3	Do-now	10 min.	Open-syllable word search
	Day 3 or 4	Independent Practice	10 min.	Open-syllable crossword puzzle
	Day 4	Do-now	10 min.	Two-syllable word prompts
	Day 4	Extension	10 min.	CV/CVC syllable word cards
	Day 5	Do-now	10 min.	Three-syllable word prompts
	Day 5	Post-test	20 min.	Post-test—CV

Week 2

Do-now

Brainstorm as many consonant–vowel combinations as you can that form actual words.

Possible Answers: go, be, hi, he, try, sly, pry, so, she, we

Mini-lesson Chapter 3: CV syllable chart

- **Time:** Fifteen minutes on one day.
- **Goal:** To develop an understanding of CV syllables and the sounds for the vowel "y."
- **Materials:** CV syllable chart, white board, dry erase markers.
- **Overview:** Working in pairs, students will spell CV words independently.

Directions

Now it is time to introduce the next type of syllable, the CV or open syllable. This syllable can form a one-syllable word or be found as a syllable in larger words. Write the following CV words on the board: "he," "she," "go," and "shy." Have students determine what the words have in common. They should notice that each word ends with a vowel and the vowel makes the long sound. Identify the rule that when the vowel sound is the last sound in a syllable, the vowel has the long sound. Have students work in pairs to write down as many one-syllable CV words with a long vowel sound as they can in three minutes. This will allow students to talk about the pattern and generate some of their own examples. If students give examples of words like "to" that are composed of a consonant vowel combination without a long vowel sound, explain that these words are exceptions to the rule.

Remind students that when determining the type of syllable, the position of the vowel is important. Students need to focus on the vowel rather than the consonants. The initial consonant can be left off or additional consonants can be added, but only at the beginning of the syllable. A change in the number of initial consonants does not change the vowel sound. Also, remind students that the long vowel says its name and that the CV syllable will typically have the long vowel sound.

Explain that the letter "y" at the end of a syllable can make two different sounds. Divide the board in half and write the word "pretty" on one half and the word "try" on the other half. Ask students to identify the sound that the y makes in each word. They will notice that the "y" makes a long /i/ sound at the end of a first syllable and a long /e/ sound at the end of other syllables.

Give each pair of students a white board and a dry erase marker. Paper can be used if white boards are not available. Dictate a syllable from the chart on the following page. Have pairs of students quickly write their answers on the boards. When time is called, have students hold up their boards. This enables you to easily read the students' responses.

CV syllable chart

ti or ty	bre	she	mu
spo	pre	ply	sta
fly	try	shy	dry
sky	by	pry	fi or fy
my	fla	fra	spy

Day 2

Do-now

Chapter 3:
Syllable matching list

Match a syllable in the first column with a syllable in the second column to make a real word.

Syllable matching list

Column 1	Column 2	Answers
pu	ping	pupil
so	man	sofa
stu	sist	student
pre	pil	pretend
fi	ro	final
mu	nal	mutate
ho	fa	hoping
re	tend	resist
he	tate	hero
ro	dent	Roman

Guided Practice

- **Time:** Fifteen minutes on one day.
- **Goal:** To develop an understanding of CV syllables.
- **Materials:** CV two-syllable word chart, white board, dry erase markers.
- **Overview:** Working in pairs, students will spell initial CV syllables of longer words.

Directions

Divide the students into pairs. Using the chart below, dictate one two-syllable word with a CV syllable in the initial position. Pairs of students work together to write the first syllable of the word on their white board. When you call time, all students hold up their boards at the same time. Pairs who get the syllable correct earn one point. Students put a tally mark in the corner of their board and then erase the syllable. You dictate the next word and the process continues. The pair with the most points is the winner.

CV two-syllable word chart

begin	demon	final	lotus	migrant
hoping	profess	program	putrid	repack
recall	token	robot	woken	basin
pupil	plywood	hydrant	student	python

Explain that if the CV syllable is in the middle of a word with three or more syllables, the vowel will sometimes have the short sound. If using the long vowel sound for the CV syllable does not create a word the student recognizes then it would be appropriate to try a short sound. For example: movable, television, chandelier, and inoculate. (Notice that in the word inoculate there are two open syllables, one with a long vowel sound and one with a short vowel sound.)

Game—Reaching the Pot of Gold

Chapter 3: Pot of Gold game board
Chapter 3: Pot of Gold syllable cards

Note: You can do this exercise on either Day 2 or 3.

- **Time:** Ten minutes on one day.
- **Goal:** To read CV and CVC syllables.
- **Materials:** Pot of Gold game board, Pot of Gold syllable cards, die, game markers.
- **Overview:** Three to five students will read CVC and CV syllables in an attempt to be the first player to reach the finish line.
- **Objective:** To be the first player to move all the way around the board by pronouncing the long or short vowel syllable on the card.

Directions

1. The dealer shuffles the syllable cards and places them in a single pile face down on the table.
2. The players roll a die and the player with the highest number goes first. The play moves clockwise around the circle.
3. The player picks up the first card and pronounces the syllable on the card.
4. If the player does not correctly pronounce the syllable, his turn is over.
5. If the player pronounces the syllable correctly, her turn continues.
6. If the syllable on the card has a short vowel sound, the player moves one space on the board. If the syllable has a long vowel sound, the player moves two spaces.
7. If the player can say a multisyllabic word that contains the syllable on the card, he gets to move one extra space during her turn.
8. The first player to make it all the way around the board is the winner.
9. As students become more confident with the words, the difficulty can be increased by requiring the player to write the syllable that is dictated by another player, rather than just reading the syllable card she draws.

Day 3

Do-now

Chapter 3:
Open-syllable word search

Find the open-syllable "words" in the following word search:

M	F	F	Z	P	I	P	P
K	G	A	P	E	S	H	I
J	M	E	P	Y	H	G	O
T	O	M	C	R	Y	G	N
N	O	D	Y	D	S	O	X
F	Y	E	V	R	O	B	E
Y	Y	T	H	Y	S	N	E
C	M	J	S	H	E	K	W

Open-syllable word search

Answers

be
my
cry
no
do
pi
dry
she
go
shy
he
so
hi
to
me
we

Independent Practice

Chapter 3:
Open-syllable crossword puzzle

Note: You can do this exercise on either Day 3 or Day 4.

- **Time:** Ten minutes on one day.
- **Goal:** Using clues, students will determine words containing specified open syllables in the initial, medial, and final positions.
- **Materials:** Open-syllable crossword puzzle.
- **Overview:** Individual or paired students complete the crossword puzzle containing open syllable words.

Answers

Across		Down	
1.	baby	2.	bingo
5.	acorn	3.	crater
8.	microphone	4.	lion
9.	concentration	6.	return
13.	open	7.	hippopotamus
14.	triangle	10.	egret
15.	poet	11.	trampoline
		12.	release

Open-syllable crossword puzzle

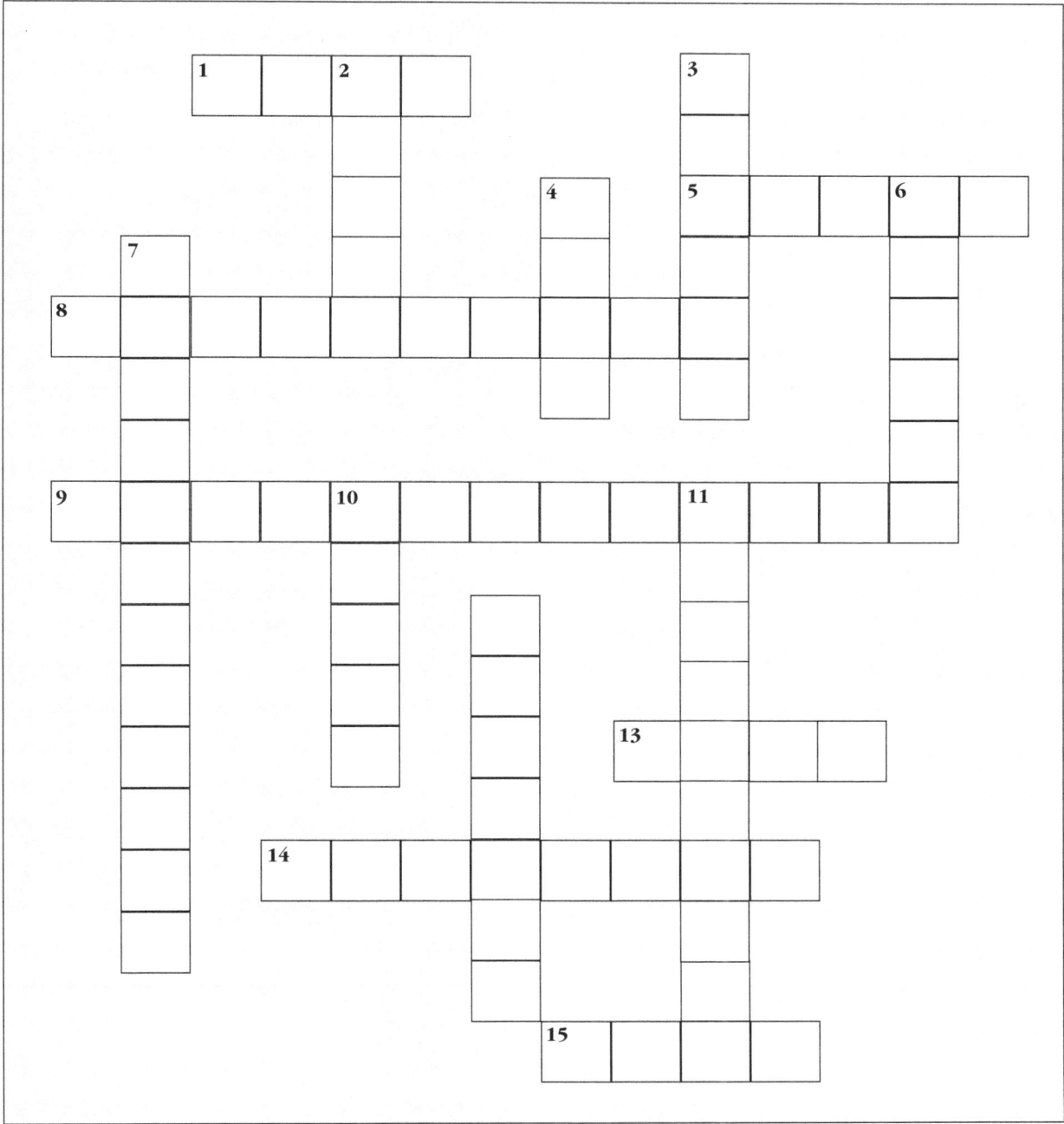

ACROSS

1. A two-syllable word that is another name for an infant

5. A two-syllable word naming the nut of an oak tree; the first syllable, "a," is open

8. A three-syllable word for an instrument used in recording or transmitting sound; the second syllable, "cro," is open

9. A four-syllable word meaning attention to one object or close mental attention; the third syllable, "tra," is open

13. A two-syllable word meaning the opposite of closed; the first syllable, "o," is open

14. A three-syllable word naming a polygon with three sides; the first syllable, "tri," is open

15. A two-syllable word naming a maker of verses; the first syllable, "po," is open

DOWN

2. A two-syllable word describing a game played on a card where the winner is the first to cover five squares in a row; the second syllable, "go," is open

3. A two-syllable word meaning a cup-shaped depression on the surface of the earth; the first syllable, "cra," is open

4. A two-syllable word for a large, heavily-built social cat; the first syllable, "li," is open

6. A two-syllable word meaning to bring back; with the first syllable, "re," is open

7. A five-syllable word naming a very large mammal with a very large head and mouth; the second syllable, "po," is open

10. A two-syllable word naming a bird with long plumes; the first syllable, "e," is open

11. A three-syllable word naming a springy, bouncy device for jumping; the second syllable, "po," is open

12. A two-syllable word meaning to let go; the first syllable, "re," is open

Day 4

Do-now

Chapter 3:
Two-syllable word prompts

Two-syllable word prompts

Directions

Look at the open syllables below. Add a second syllable of your choice to form a two-syllable word. If you can't think of a second syllable to form a word, look in the dictionary and try to find one that has the word you selected as its first syllable. If it is a word you don't know, define it.

Examples:
Go: Goanna—any of several large Australian monitor lizards

Be: Benign—showing kindness and gentleness

1. Co
2. De
3. Di
4. Gri
5. Le
6. Pre

When the class is ready, have students share new words and their definitions.

Extension

Chapter 3:
CV/CVC syllable word cards

- **Time:** Ten minutes on one day.
- **Goal:** To read CV and CVC syllable cards.
- **Materials:** CV/CVC syllable word cards.
- **Overview:** Two to twenty students determine the syllable type and combine their cards to make two-syllable words.

Directions

Each student is given a card with a CV or CVC syllable on it. A CV label is placed on one side of the board and a CVC label is on the other. The students then stand in the area designated for their type of syllable. Each student reads his syllable to the class.

The teacher collects all the cards and redistributes them one per student. The students circulate around the room and find a syllable that can be combined with their new syllable to make a two-syllable word. Each pair of students writes the word they formed on the classroom white board and reads it to the class.

CV/CVC syllable word cards

fi	nal	pu	trid	mi
grant	pro	fess	hy	drant
ro	dent	re	sist	wo
ken	re	call	be	gin

Day 5

Do-now Chapter 3:
Three-syllable word prompts

Three-syllable word prompts

Directions

Look at the open syllables below. Choose three of the first syllables from the list below and add two syllables of your choice to form a three-syllable word. If you can't form a word, look in the dictionary and try to find one that has the word you selected as its first syllable. If it is a word you don't know, define it.

Example: Co: Coexist—to live in peace

1. de
2. di
3. gri
4. le
5. pre
6. go
7. be

When the class is ready, have students share new words and their definitions.

Indicate how many syllables are in each word. If the word can be divided into syllables, indicate how it is divided.

Example: hero   <u>2 he * ro</u>

1. slepo   _____

2. cribu   _____

3. ibo   _____

4. graboti   _____

5. etamo   _____

6. thra   _____

7. brenu   _____

8. shre   _____

9. thabo   _____

10. plibato   _____

Write the words that your teacher dictates for each question.

1. _____   6. _____

2. _____   7. _____

3. _____   8. _____

4. _____   9. _____

5. _____   10. _____

Read the following passage orally.

The Ba and the Shebo

A ba, crossing a thre over a fluta with a piece of cra in his nymu, saw his own shebo in the bruti and took it for that of another ba, with a ple of cra double his own in size. He immediately let go of his ply, and fiercely attacked the other ba to get his larger ple from him. He cro lost both: that which he grasped at in the bruti, because it was a shebo; and his ply, because the fluta swept it away.

Answers

1. slepo   <u>2   sle * po</u>
2. cribu   <u>2   cri * bu</u>
3. ibo   <u>2   i * bo</u>
4. graboti   <u>3   gra * bo * ti</u>
5. etamo   <u>3   e * ta * mo</u>
6. thra   <u>1   thra</u>
7. brenu   <u>2   bre * nu</u>
8. shre   <u>1   shre</u>
9. thabo   <u>2   tha * bo</u>
10. plibato   <u>3   pli * ba * to</u>

1. fla		6. igu	
2. truba		7. jeba	
3. shibo		8. siba	
4. imu		9. gletu	
5. thre		10. sani	

The Ba and the She * bo

A <u>ba</u>, crossing a <u>thre</u> over a <u>flu * ta</u> with a piece of <u>cra</u> in his <u>ny * mu</u>, saw his own <u>she * bo</u> in the <u>bru * ti</u> and took it for that of another <u>ba</u>, with a <u>ple</u> of <u>cra</u> double his own in size. He immediately let go of his <u>ply</u>, and fiercely attacked the other <u>ba</u> to get his larger <u>ple</u> from him. He <u>cro</u> lost both: that which he grasped at in the <u>bru * ti</u>, because it was a <u>she * bo</u>; and his <u>ply</u>, because the <u>flu * ta</u> swept it away.

Scoring: Number of underlined words correct   /20

Chap·ter 4
CVC & CV Syllables

Sequence	Suggested Time Frame	Moving to Automaticity	Time	Materials
Week 3: CVC/CV	Day 1	Do-now	10 min.	Syllable matching list
	Day 1	Mini-lesson	10 min.	Syllable sort graphic organizer, syllable sort cards, class white board
	Day 2	Do-now	10 min.	Syllable fill-in-the-blanks
	Day 2	Mini-lesson from Day 1 cont'd.	10 min.	Syllable sort graphic organizer, syllable sort cards, class white board
	Day 3	Do-now	10 min.	CV syllable prompts
	Day 3	Guided Practice	15 min.	White boards and dry erase markers, lists A and B
	Day 4	Do-now	10 min.	Medial syllables prompts
	Day 4	Game— Syllable Memory	10 min.	Syllable memory cards
	Day 4	Independent Practice	10 min.	CV/CVC worksheet
	Day 5	Do-now	10 min.	Nonsense word prompts
	Day 5	Post-test	20 min.	Post-test—CV/CVC

Week 3

Day 1

Do-now

Chapter 4:
Syllable matching list

Syllable matching list

Form a three-syllable word by combining one syllable from each column. Remember that medial CV syllables can have long or short vowel sounds.

Syllables			Answers
rep	i	dent	rep * re * sent
oc	pu	pus	oc * to * pus
com	to	ment	com * pu * ter
ev	ti	sent	ev * i * dent
sen	re	ter	sen * ti * ment

Mini-lesson

Chapter 4: Syllable sort graphic organizer
Chapter 4: Syllable sort cards

Note: This lesson can take place on Days 1 and 2.
- **Time:** Ten minutes on two days.
- **Goal:** To develop an understanding of how to divide words containing CVC and CV syllables.
- **Materials:** Syllable sort graphic organizer, syllable sort cards, class white board.
- **Overview:** Working in pairs, students practice dividing words into syllables.

Directions

Explain to students that since they have learned about the CVC and CV syllables, they are ready to start combining these to form longer words. However, they will need to learn the rules to help them determine the vowel sound in each syllable. Mastering these rules will help with both encoding and decoding.

Write the following multisyllabic nonsense word on the board: "brematbufin." Have students guess what they think the pronunciation is, but do not confirm it. Tell them you will come back to this again at the end of the lesson. First, they are going to discover the rule.

The purpose of teaching phonics is to help students move an unknown word into a recognizable word. If the word is not already in a student's listening vocabulary, phonics will not help her make meaning of the word. Helping students understand the phonics rules will help bring together their listening and reading vocabularies and improve their comprehension. It can be important to explain a phonics rule to students, but sometimes it is more effective if they discover the rule themselves.

Tell your students you are going to use a syllable sort to help them discover the rule. Make a copy of the following chart on an overhead sheet. Write the words on the overhead sheet or have them already copied onto a sheet of overhead film. Cut the words apart so that you can display one word at a time.

Begin by placing the first few words in the appropriate sections. Answers are included for your convenience. As students start to discover the pattern, ask individual students to place a word in the section where it belongs.

Syllable sort graphic organizer

Divide between Two Consonants CVC * CVC	Divide before the Consonant CV * CVC	Divide after the Consonant CVC * VC

Syllable sort cards

victim	zenith	topic
velvet	topaz	habit
muffin	relent	cabin
talcum	spoken	polish
goblin	totem	present
witness	omit	seven
tonsil	focus	contest
cactus	human	pupil
tablet	bonus	crisis
candid	moment	rabid

The students should discover that when there are two consonants between the vowels, you usually divide between the consonants. When there is one consonant between the vowels, it is more common to divide before the consonant and make the first vowel long. However, if that does not make a word they know, the students should divide after the first consonant and make the vowel in the first syllable short.

Once students have discovered the rule, guided practice should begin with words containing two CVC syllables. Write the word "tunnel" on the board. Teach students to first underline the vowels in the word to determine the number of syllables. If there are two vowels, students count the number of consonants between the vowels. If there are two consonants between the vowel sounds, divide between the consonants.

For example, the first step in the word "tunnel" would be to underline the vowels—*tunnel*. There are two vowel sounds, so there are two syllables in the word. Between the underlined vowels there are two consonants, two "n's." Students should divide the word into two parts between the "n's." The first syllable would then be "tun," and the second would be "nel." Students have now determined that the word contains two CVC syllables. Based on their understanding of CVC syllables, students know that the vowel sound in each syllable is most likely short.

If students were to discover that there is just one consonant between the two vowels, they would divide before the consonant. This would produce one CV syllable having a long vowel sound and one CVC syllable having a short vowel sound. If this does not produce a word that they know, students would then try dividing the word after the consonant, making the first vowel sound short.

Syllable sort answers

Divide between Two Consonants CVC * CVC	Divide before the Consonant CV * CVC	Divide after the Consonant CVC * VC
victim	zenith	topic
velvet	topaz	habit
muffin	relent	cabin
talcum	spoken	polish
goblin	totem	present
witness	omit	seven
tonsil	focus	contest
cactus	human	pupil
tablet	bonus	crisis
candid	moment	rabid

Day 2

Syllable fill-in-the-blanks

The words in the box below are divided into syllables. Combine the syllables to determine the word. Use the words to complete the sentences.

min * is * ter	cus * to * mer	ac * ro * bat
van * ish * ing	vi * ta * min	fan * tas * tic
rec * om * mend		

1. The _____ walked on the high wire during the circus.

2. I take a _____ once a day to make sure that I am getting all the nutrition I need.

3. The magician had a trick that used a _____ rabbit.

4. The _____ bought paint and paintbrushes at the hardware store.

5. That dinner you fixed was _____.

6. The _____ officiated during the wedding ceremony.

7. I would _____ that you travel lightly so you don't have to pay for extra luggage.

Answers

1. ac * ro * bat
2. vi * ta * min
3. van * ish * ing
4. cus * to * mer
5. fan * tas * tic
6. min * is * ter
7. rec * om * mend

Mini-lesson

Continue from Day 1.

Day 3

Do-now
Chapter 4:
CV syllable prompts

CV syllable prompts

Write the medial CV syllable of each word and indicate whether the vowel in the medial syllable makes a long or a short sound.

Prompts	Answers
President	si—short
Vibration	bra—long
Volcano	ca—long
Qualify	li—short
Comedy	me—short
Difficult	fi—short

Guided Practice
Chapter 4:
Lists A and B

- **Time:** Fifteen minutes on one day.
- **Goal:** To practice dividing words containing CV and CVC syllables.
- **Materials:** White boards and dry erase markers, lists A and B.
- **Overview:** Paired students dictate, write, and check multisyllabic words.

Directions

Divide the class in pairs. Give one member of each pair Chart A and the other member Chart B. The first student dictates his words to the second student, who writes them on the white board. Then student two dictates her words to student one, who also writes them on the white board. Then they check each other's list for accuracy.

List A	List B
nomad	virus
protect	yoga
racket	insect
digest	human
magnetic	hypnosis

Write the following nonsense words on the board and have each pair of students attempt to decode the words. After they have had an opportunity to pronounce each word, discuss as a class each step for decoding the words.

tramtep (Answer: tram * tep)

1. Underline the vowels. There are two.
2. Count the number of consonants between the vowels. There are two.
3. Divide between the consonants, so the first vowel is short.
4. The second syllable ends with a consonant, so it has a second short vowel.

obstrantum (Answer: ob * stran * tum)

1. Underline the vowels. There are three.
2. Count the number of consonants between the first two vowels. There are four.
3. Do any of those consonants typically form blends? Yes, "str" does. So divide between the b and the s.
4. Count the number of consonants between the second and third vowels. There are two.
5. Divide between the consonants, so the second syllable is closed and the vowel is short.
6. The third syllable ends with a consonant, so it closed and has a short third vowel sound.

dodefin (Answer: do * def * in)

1. Underline the vowels. There are three.
2. Count the number of consonants between the first two vowels. There is one.
3. When there is one consonant, divide before it. This would make the first vowel long.
4. Remind students that if this were not a nonsense word they would check to make sure that the word was recognizable. If it were not, then they would try the short vowel sound to form a recognizable word.
5. Count the number of consonants between the second and the third vowels. There is one.
6. Because the next syllable is a medial syllable, try the short sound first. If this were not a nonsense word the next step would be to try the long vowel sound.
7. The third syllable ends with a consonant, so it has a short sound.

To practice this skill with an actual word, write the word "hippopotamus" on the board. Paired students can divide the word into syllables and identify whether the medial vowel sounds are long or short.

Discuss with students the steps involved in determining the pronunciation of the word they examined at the beginning of the lesson:

brematbufin (Answer: bre * mat * bu * fin)

1. Underline the vowel combinations and identify the number of syllables. There are four.
2. Determine the number of consonants between each of the vowels. There is one consonant between the first and second vowels, two between the second and third vowels, one between the third and fourth vowels, and one after the fourth.
3. Divide the first two syllables before the "m." There is only one consonant between the vowels, so try the long vowel sound first.
4. The second vowel should have a short sound because it has two consonants after it. Divide between the consonants.
5. The next one is tricky. There is only one consonant after the vowel, but because it is a longer word (four syllables) try the short vowel sound. Since this is a nonsense word, we cannot use our listening vocabulary to help us. The "u" could be short or long.
6. The final vowel would be short because there is a consonant that closes the syllable.

Day 4

Do-now

Chapter 4:
Medial syllables prompts

Medial syllables prompts

Add one of the medial syllables below to each word and then use the word in a sentence.

den   ta   i   as   pel

Prompts	**Answers**
1. pro_____ler	propeller
2. gar ____er	gardener
3. vi____min	vitamin
4. ven__son	venison
5. dis____ter	disaster

Sentences will vary.

Game—Syllable Memory

Chapter 4:
Syllable memory cards

- **Time:** Ten minutes on one day.
- **Goal:** To combine syllables to make real two-syllable words.
- **Materials:** Syllable memory cards.
- **Overview:** Two to three players take turns flipping over two syllable memory cards at a time to combine them to form a real word. The person with the most matches is the winner.
- **Objective:** To form more two-syllable words than your opponent.

Directions

1. The dealer shuffles the cards and places each card face down on the table.
2. The first player turns over two cards. The player combines the cards to form a single word by reading the syllables together. The player needs to try each card as both the first and the last syllable of the word.
3. If the cards form a word, the player keeps the match and gets to go again.
4. If the syllables do not form a word, the cards are returned to their spaces on the table and it is the next player's turn.
5. Play continues until all possible matches are found.
6. Some of the cards might not be used because syllables can be combined in various ways to form different words.
7. The game ends when all possible words have been made.

Independent Practice

Chapter 4:
CV/CVC worksheet

- **Time:** Ten minutes on one day.
- **Goal:** To become proficient recognizing syllables in a given word.
- **Materials:** CV/CVC worksheet.
- **Overview:** Individually, students determine the number of syllables in a given word and use the words in a written response.

CV/CVC worksheet

Directions

Underline the vowels in each word. Count the number of consonants between the vowels. If there are two consonants, divide between the consonants. If there is one consonant, decide whether to divide before or after the consonant.

napkin	planet
robin	comet
hobbit	bonus
hoping	hopping
lavish	velvet
hero	helmet
catnip	whiplash
pupil	student
tendon	timid
after	talcum
index	kingdom

Create a story using at least ten of the above words and write it on the lines below.

_____

_____

_____

_____

_____

_____

_____

_____

_____

_____

_____

_____

Answers

napkin	nap kin		planet	plan et
robin	rob in		comet	com et
hobbit	hob bit		bonus	bo nus
hoping	ho ping		hopping	hop ping
lavish	lav ish		velvet	vel vet
hero	he ro		helmet	hel met
catnip	cat nip		whiplash	whip lash
pupil	pu pil		student	stu dent
tendon	ten don		timid	tim id
after	af ter		talcum	tal cum
index	in dex		kingdom	king dom

Create a story using at least ten of the above words and write it on the lines below.

Answers will vary.

Day 5

Do-now
Chapter 4:
Nonsense word prompts

Nonsense word prompts
Divide each of the nonsense words into syllables.

Nonsense Words	Answers
rebinnot	re * bin * not
strummet	strum * met
conthustic	con * thus * tic
unflenel	un * fle * nel
identisop	i * den * ti * sop

Create a nonsense word to match each of the patterns below.

CV * CVC

CVC * CVC

Post-test—CV and CVC

Indicate how many syllables are in each word. If the word can be divided into syllables, indicate how it is divided.

Example: tulip   2   tu * lip

1. rebontrep _____

2. sodinnemtun _____

3. nymbopi _____

4. vofin _____

5. quabus _____

6. strumvetnim _____

7. rabemmef _____

8. frotin _____

9. synnafis _____

10. brontestant _____

Write the words that your teacher dictates for each question.

1. _____   6. _____

2. _____   7. _____

3. _____   8. _____

4. _____   9. _____

5. _____   10. _____

Read the following passage orally.

The Stepo and the Crebbento

A stepo one day crammetted the flom fet and slop plabam of the crebbento, who repvid, laughing: "Though you be sweft as the wend, I will bret you in a racet." The stepo, believing her assenton to be simply impossiblen, assented to the fropisil, and they agreed that the plix should choose the cons and fix the gont.

On the day appinted for the racet the two started together. The crebbento nevet for a moment stopped, but went on with a slo but steddy plagam strat to the end of the cons. The stepo, lying down by the wapsip, fell fast asleep. At last waking up, and miving as fast as he could, he saw the crebbento had reached the gont, and was comfotably dozing afyot her fatgum.

Answers

1. rebontrep   __3__   re * bon * trep   or   reb * on * trep
2. sodinnemtun   __4__   so * din * nem * tun   or   sod * in * nem * tun
3. nymbopi   __3__   nym * bo * pi   or   nym * bop * i
4. vofin   __2__   vo * fin   or   vof * in
5. quabus   __2__   qua * bus   or   quab * us
6. strumvetnim   __3__   strum * vet * nim
7. rabemmef   __3__   ra * bem * mef   or   rab * em * mef
8. frotin   __2__   fro * tin   or   frot * in
9. synnafis   __3__   syn * na * fis   or   syn * naf * is
10. brontestant   __3__   bron * tes * tant

1. fla * ten
2. trub * an * ti
3. shi * bo * trum
4. im * mut
5. thre * po

6. i * gun * tep
7. jeb * ba
8. se * bat
9. gle * top
10. san * tip

The Ste * po and the Creb * ben * to

A ste * po one day cram * met * ted the flom fet and slop pla * bam of the creb * ben * to, who rep * vid, laughing: "Though you be sweft as the wend, I will bret you in a ra * cet." The ste * po, believing her as * sen * ton to be sim * ply im * pos * sib * len, as * sen * ted to the fro * pi * sil, and they agreed that the plix should choose the cons and fix the gont.

On the day ap * pin * ted for the ra * cet the two started together. The creb * ben * to ne * vet for a mo * ment stopped, but went on with a slo but sted * dy pla * gam strat to the end of the cons. The ste * po, ly * ing down by the wap * sip, fell fast asleep. At last wa * king up, and mi * ving as fast as he could, he saw the creb * ben * to had reached the gont, and was com * fo * tab * ly do * zing af * yot her fat * gum.

Scoring: Number of underlined words correct   /43

Chap·ter 5
Cle Syllable

Sequence	Concept and Suggested Time Frame	Moving to Automaticity	Time	Materials
Week 4: Cle syllable	Day 1	Do-now	10 min.	
	Day 1	Mini-lesson	15 min.	Cle syllable graphic organizer, Cle syllable sort cards
	Day 2	Do-now	10 min.	ABC sort
	Day 2	Guided practice	20 min.	Individual white boards, dry erase markers, Cle word chart
	Day 3	Do-now	10 min.	Cle fill-in-the-blanks
	Day 3 or 4	Extension	15 min.	Baseball memory cards, classroom baseball diamond
	Day 4	Do-now	10 min.	
	Day 4	Independent practice	15 min.	Syllable chart, small blank cards
	Day 4	Game— Baseball	20 min.	Baseball memory cards, classroom baseball diamond
	Day 5	Do-now	10 min.	Cle word search
	Day 5	Post-test	20 min.	Post-test—Cle

Week 4

Day 1

Do-now

Make a list of as many words with a Cle syllable as you can.

Mini-lesson

Chapter 5: Cle syllable graphic organizer
Chapter 5: Cle syllable sort cards

- **Time:** Fifteen minutes on one day.
- **Goal:** To develop an understanding of the Cle syllable and how it impacts the syllable preceding it.
- **Materials:** Cle syllable graphic organizer, Cle syllable sort cards.
- **Overview:** Students determine the rules for decoding words containing the Cle syllable.

Directions

Display the following graphic organizer on the overhead. Place the words "han * dle" and "gig * gle" in the left-hand box and the word "ri * fle" in the right-hand box. Have the students try to determine the rule for the final syllable and how it impacts the vowel sound in the initial syllable. Students should identify that the consonant immediately preceding the "le" goes with the "le" to form the final syllable. This will determine whether the initial syllable is open or closed and whether the vowel sound is long or short.

Cle syllable graphic organizer

Cle Syllable

Have students decide which box each of the words below belongs in. This will help students generate the rule. They will observe that all the words end with "le." Then give students five minutes to work with a partner to identify additional Cle words and place them in the appropriate box on the graphic organizer.

Cle syllable sort cards

pic * kle	fa * ble	mus * cle
hob * ble	pud * dle	thim * ble
Bi * ble	hum * ble	sta * ple

As students are working they should observe two characteristics. In each case, the Cle syllable is found as the final syllable of the word. The syllable contains a consonant before the "le." This explains why the word "rifle" is spelled "rifle" rather than "riffle." The "le" takes the consonant before it in the Cle syllable, so the initial syllable becomes a CV syllable and has a long vowel sound. Developing this understanding will help students encode and decode many additional words.

Explain that, however, in some words, like giggle and handle, there are two consonants before the "le." They can either be the same consonant or two different consonants. When the "le" takes the consonant right before it, there is still one consonant left to close the first syllable. Closing the syllable makes the first syllable have a short vowel sound and it is a CVC syllable.

Day 2

Do-now

Chapter 5: ABC sort

Working in pairs, fill in the ABC sort. In each box write at least one word that begins with one of the designated letters and contains a Cle syllable.

ABC sort

ABC	DEF	GHI
JKL	MN	OPQ
RS	TUV	WXYZ

Guided Practice

Chapter 5: Cle word chart

- **Time:** Twenty minutes on one day.
- **Goal:** To develop proficiency encoding words with Cle syllables.
- **Materials:** Individual white boards, dry erase markers, Cle word chart.
- **Overview:** Teacher dictates Cle words and pairs of students write those words in syllables on individual white boards.

Directions

With the practice of dividing words into syllables, students will begin to understand how the placement of the consonants within a word affects the preceding vowel sound. Using individual white boards, students work with partners to write in syllables the Cle word the teacher dictates. For example, the word "cable" would be written "ca * ble." After each word when time is called, students hold up their boards. A point is awarded to each pair of students who have the correct answer. Students keep a record of their points on their white board. The pair with the most points at the end of the practice wins. Words for dictation are listed on the next page.

Cle word chart

cable	saddle	puddle	rifle	cradle
cuddle	baffle	puzzle	quibble	bridle
huddle	castle	giggle	guzzle	Bible
riddle	hustle	drizzle	fable	stable
muffle	cripple	crumble	stumble	handle
middle	babble	bustle	bubble	table

Practice should continue until students exhibit proficiency.

Day 3

Do-now   Chapter 5: Cle fill-in-the-blanks

Cle fill-in-the-blanks

Complete each sentence with a word containing a Cle syllable.

1. To keep from pricking my finger when I am sewing I use a _____.
2. The tow truck attached a _____ to the car so that it could be towed behind the truck.
3. The _____ was put on the horse to lead it around the rink.
4. He put a pillow over his head to _____ the noise in the room so that he could sleep.
5. I know that the little child will _____ during the long speech.
6. Every man's home is considered his _____ even if it is just a cottage.

Answers

1. thimble   2. cable   3. bridle   4. muffle   5. wiggle   6. castle

Extension   Chapter 5: Baseball memory cards

Note: You can do this exercise on either Day 3 or 4.
- **Time:** Fifteen minutes on one day.
- **Goal:** To develop proficiency encoding words with Cle syllables that contain prefixes and suffixes.
- **Materials:** Baseball memory cards, classroom baseball diamond.
- **Overview:** Pitcher dictates Cle words and students earn runs by spelling Cle words with prefixes or suffixes correctly.

Directions

As students become more proficient, this game may be adapted to allow students to steal a base. Only the batter can steal. A steal must be announced before the ball is "pitched." To steal a base, the batter must add a prefix or a suffix to the pitched word and spell the entire word correctly. Adding a prefix or a suffix would add one base to the batter's turn. Adding both a prefix and a suffix would add two bases. In either case, correct prefixes and suffixes must be used and the word must be spelled correctly, or the batter is out.

Day 4

Do-now

In English there are ten consonants that can typically begin a Cle syllable. List the typical Cle syllables and give an example of a word containing each.

Answers

ble—bramble	cle—uncle	ckle—tickle	dle—handle	zle—puzzle
fle—rifle	gle—wiggle	ple—maple	tle—settle	stle—castle

Independent Practice   Chapter 5: Syllable chart

- **Time:** Fifteen minutes on one day.
- **Goal:** To develop proficiency encoding syllables, identifying the types, and combining syllables to form real words.
- **Materials:** Syllable chart, small blank cards.
- **Overview:** Students encode, classify, and combine syllables.

Directions

Dictate the syllables below and have students write them on small cards. Have them put a different syllable on each card. Using these cards, students work with a partner to divide the cards by syllable types: CVC, CV, or Cle. This will give the students practice identifying and reading the three types of syllables.

Syllable chart

roc	ket	cat	tle	he
ro	ca	ble	bat	tle
con	tact	fin	ish	mi
nus	hu	mid	su	per
wig	gle	pre	vent	pho
ny	py	thon	sta	ple

Using these cards, students can play a memory game. Students spread their cards face-down on the desk. The first student turns over two cards. If these syllables can be combined to form a two-syllable word, the student reads the word and keeps the cards. She then takes another turn. If the cards cannot be combined to form a real word, the student turns the cards back over, and it is the next player's turn. The student who has made the most words at the end of the game is the winner.

Game—Baseball

Chapter 5:
Baseball memory cards

- **Time:** Twenty minutes on one day.
- **Goal:** To develop proficiency encoding words with Cle syllables.
- **Materials:** Baseball memory cards, classroom baseball diamond.
- **Overview:** Pitcher dictates Cle words and students earn runs by spelling Cle words correctly.
- **Objective:** To earn more runs than the other team by identifying the correct spelling of the pitched word.
- **Classroom Setup:** Create a baseball diamond in your classroom. You will need a home plate, first base, second base, and third base. You will also need a scoreboard.

Directions

1. Divide the class into two teams.
2. Flip a coin to see which team goes first.
3. The team that goes first sends one of their members to be the first "batter."
4. A designated "pitcher" from the other team randomly selects a card from the pile of baseball cards and reads it to the batter.
5. The batter orally indicates how many consonants are between the vowel and the "le" and then spells the word.
6. If the batter spells the word correctly, the batter moves to first or second base. The base is determined by the number of consonants before the "le" in the "pitched" word. If the word has a single consonant after the vowel and before the "le" (e.g., noble, able, rifle), the batter has hit a single and goes to first base. If the word has two consonants after the vowel and before the "le" (bubble, stumble, hobble, gamble), the batter moves to second base and has hit a double.
7. Then the next batter comes to home plate. Play continues as it would in a normal baseball game. Two players may not be on the same base. The next batter may force the player "on base" to move to the next base.
8. A misspelled word would be an out. After three outs, the next team is "at bat."
9. The teacher may choose to limit the number of batters in each inning to keep the game moving.

Day 5

Do-now

Chapter 5:
Cle word search

Find ten words with Cle syllables.

Cle word search

I	F	C	T	E	E	M	M	L	T	W	R	C	H	O
R	G	A	L	Q	J	S	W	Z	I	P	E	Z	K	O
X	M	F	B	E	Q	R	H	G	R	I	L	T	T	T
C	I	O	M	L	R	H	G	M	I	C	T	I	G	L
R	N	X	Y	H	E	L	J	K	N	K	S	T	Q	L
H	X	S	R	F	E	I	X	X	J	L	A	L	T	L
H	R	M	K	E	E	U	A	H	B	E	C	E	V	I
K	U	Q	C	T	L	F	I	H	E	L	D	N	A	H
M	A	P	L	E	K	B	B	W	U	R	F	A	Z	
S	S	V	S	F	P	C	A	I	J	D	M	U	L	Q
W	E	W	B	U	A	R	O	T	O	G	D	X	P	V
N	Y	A	B	K	U	I	Z	N	S	B	W	L	L	D
N	R	M	X	V	G	R	W	J	R	T	U	L	E	C
I	N	A	J	B	Z	Z	V	Y	Y	L	M	X	M	V
N	P	L	H	S	N	B	K	Q	J	F	F	L	L	P

Answers

castle
fable
handle
huddle
maple
pickle
rifle
stable
title
wiggle

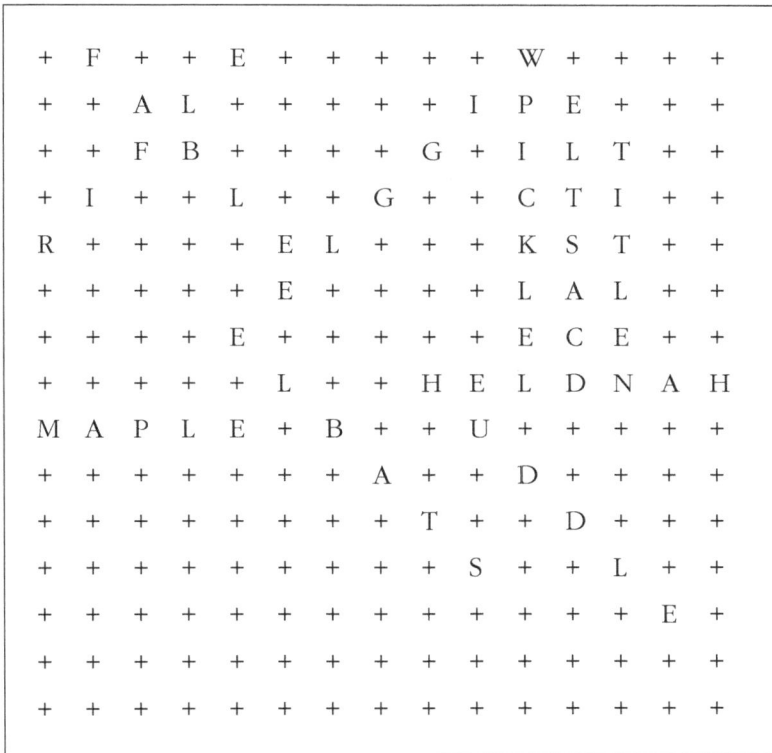

```
+  F  +  +  E  +  +  +  +  +  W  +  +  +  +
+  +  A  L  +  +  +  +  +  I  P  E  +  +  +
+  +  F  B  +  +  +  G  +  I  L  T  +  +
+  I  +  +  L  +  +  G  +  +  C  T  I  +  +
R  +  +  +  +  E  L  +  +  +  K  S  T  +  +
+  +  +  +  +  E  +  +  +  +  L  A  L  +  +
+  +  +  +  E  +  +  +  +  +  E  C  E  +  +
+  +  +  +  +  L  +  +  H  E  L  D  N  A  H
M  A  P  L  E  +  B  +  +  U  +  +  +  +  +
+  +  +  +  +  +  +  A  +  +  D  +  +  +  +
+  +  +  +  +  +  +  +  T  +  +  D  +  +  +
+  +  +  +  +  +  +  +  +  S  +  +  L  +  +
+  +  +  +  +  +  +  +  +  +  +  +  +  E  +
+  +  +  +  +  +  +  +  +  +  +  +  +  +  +
+  +  +  +  +  +  +  +  +  +  +  +  +  +  +
```

Over, Down, Direction
CASTLE (12, 7, N)
FABLE (2, 1, SE)
HANDLE (15, 8, W)
HUDDLE (9, 8, SE)
MAPLE (1, 9, E)
PICKLE (11, 2, S)
RIFLE (1, 5, NE)
STABLE (10, 12, NW)
TITLE (13, 3, S)
WIGGLE (11, 1, SW)

Indicate how many syllables are in each word. If the word can be divided into syllables, indicate how it is divided.

Example: trispen   2   tris * pen

1. strapple _____

2. pranst _____

3. thritle _____

4. driggle _____

5. constracle _____

6. blentum _____

7. quost _____

8. uncontestibble _____

9. antimogle _____

10. yetpamuc _____

Write the words that your teacher dictates for each question.

1. _____   6. _____

2. _____   7. _____

3. _____   8. _____

4. _____   9. _____

5. _____   10. _____

Read the following passage orally.

The Wagle in Stund

A wagle demanded the danter of a woodcutter in mantle. The faddle, unwilling to grant, and yet afrid to refuttle his request, hit upon this expedant to rid himself of his importunito. He expressed his willingness to accept the wagle as the suttor of his danter on one condittle: that he should inkle him to extract his preth, and cut off his clants, as his danter was fenfully afrid of both. The wagle cheerfully assented to the proposal. But when the prethless, clantless wagle retund to repet his request, the Woodman, no longer afrid, set on him with his club, and drov him away into the fobble.

Answers

1. strapple   <u>2</u>   strap * ple
2. pranst   <u>1</u>   pranst
3. thritle   <u>2</u>   thri * tle
4. driggle   <u>2</u>   drig * gle
5. constracle   <u>3</u>   con * stra * cle
6. blentum   <u>2</u>   blen * tum
7. quost   <u>1</u>   quost
8. uncontestibble   <u>5</u>   un * con * tes * tib * ble
9. antimogle   <u>4</u>   an * ti * mo * gle
10. yetpamuc   <u>3</u>   yet * pa * muc

1. fran * dle   6. slep * ple
2. con * tris * tle   7. drun * dle
3. bri * gle   8. grat * tle
4. cloz * zle   9. sis * tan
5. yub * ble   10. flog * gle

The Wa * gle in Stund

A <u>wa * gle</u> <u>de * man * ded</u> the <u>dan * ter</u> of a wood <u>cut * ter</u> in <u>man * tle</u>. The <u>fad * dle</u>, <u>un * wil * ling</u> to grant, and yet <u>af * rid</u> to <u>re * fut * tle</u> his <u>re * quest</u>, hit upon this <u>ex * pe * dant</u> to rid <u>him * self</u> of his <u>im * por * tu * ni * to</u>. He <u>ex * pres * sed</u> his <u>wil * ling * ness</u> to <u>ac * cept</u> the <u>wa * gle</u> as the <u>sut * tor</u> of his <u>dan * ter</u> on one <u>con * dit * tle</u>: that he should <u>in * kle</u> him to <u>ex * tract</u> his <u>preth</u>, and cut off his <u>clants</u>, as his <u>dan * ter</u> was <u>fen * ful * ly</u> <u>af * rid</u> of both. The <u>wa * gle</u> <u>chen * ful * ly</u> <u>as * sen * ted</u> to the <u>pro * po * sal</u>. But when the <u>preth * less</u>, <u>clant * less</u> <u>wa * gle</u> <u>re * tund</u> to <u>re * pet</u> his <u>re * quest</u>, the wood man, no <u>lon * ger</u> <u>af * rid</u>, set on him with his club, and <u>drov</u> him away into the <u>fob * ble</u>.

Scoring: Number of underlined words correct   /42

Chap·ter 6
R-control Syllables

Sequence	Suggested Time Frame	Moving to Automaticity	Time	Materials
Week 5: R-control	Day 1	Do-now	10 min.	
	Day 1	Mini-lesson	20 min.	R-control vowel combination cards, R-control vowel word chart, white boards, dry erase markers
	Day 2	Do-now	10 min.	R-control combination prompts #1
	Day 2	Mini-lesson	20 min.	R-control vowel combination cards, R-control vowel word chart, white boards, dry erase markers
	Day 3	Do-now	10 min.	R-control combination prompts #2
	Day 3	Guided Practice	15 min.	Vocabulary graphic organizer, "Sportsmanship" story
	Day 3	Game—Pyramid Game	15 min.	Pyramid, timer
	Day 4	Do-now	10 min.	R-control fill-in-the-blanks
	Day 4	Independent Practice	15 min.	R-control vowel worksheet #1
	Day 4	Extension	15 min.	R-control vowel worksheet #2
	Day 5	Do-now	10 min.	Syllable matching list
	Day 5	Post-test	20 min.	Post-test—R-control syllables

Week 5

Day 1

Do-now

Label a sheet of paper with the five columns below. Give five examples of each type of R-control words.

AR   ER   IR   OR   UR

Answers will vary.

Mini-lesson

Chapter 6: R-control vowel combination cards
Chapter 6: R-control vowel word chart

Note: You can do this lesson on both Days 1 and 2.
- **Time:** Twenty minutes on two days.
- **Goal:** To develop proficiency identifying R-control vowels.
- **Materials:** R-control vowel combination cards, R-control vowel word chart, white boards, dry erase markers.
- **Overview:** Students identify the R-control vowel combinations and syllables in dictated words.

Directions

Explain to students that the R-control syllables are those that have the letter "R" after the vowel. The "R" changes the sound that the vowel makes so it is neither long nor short. It makes a different sound.

Most students do not experience too much difficulty reading the R-control syllables because the R-control syllables can only make three sounds; the /ar/, /er/, or /or/ rather than five. The "er," "ir," and "ur" combinations all make the same sound. For this reason encoding the /er/ sound is more difficult than reading it. Students will need practice encoding these words before they reach the automatic level.

Each student gets the five R-control vowel combination cards below. The teacher reads a word from the chart. Each student holds up the card that would be used in the spelling of the word. Students earn one point for each word they answer correctly. The student with the most points at the end of the game is the winner.

R-control vowel word chart

carton	chirp	porch	charm	force	transport
storm	starlight	pork	morning	another	doctor
curl	carpenter	cherish	percussion	born	burn
thorn	carpet	finger	furnish	plaster	organ
carnival	chapter	motor	crater	copper	card
garble	cardinal	hurdle	skirt	shirt	dirt

Students also need to be aware that the letter "w" before the vowel can change the sound that the vowel makes. The letter "w" changes the /ar/ sound to the /or/ sound, and it changes the /or/ sound to the /er/ sound. Examples of R-control vowel words beginning with "w" are provided below.

war	worst	warm	ward	worst	wart
worm	awkward	forward	backward	warn	word

In a two-syllable word, the "r" usually goes with the vowel before it. Dictate the words below. Have students work in pairs, write the words, and divide them into syllables on small white boards.

morn * ing	car * ni * val	hur * dle	ad * mir * a * tion
fur * nish	cir * cum * fer * ence	car * ton	per * spir * a * tion
bar * ter	cir * cle	gar * ble	car * din * al
cir * cu * la * tion	as * pir * a * tion	cur * tain	cer * tain
sir * loin	en * cir * cle	vir * tu * al	ad * mir * al
or * gan	fur * ther	car * ni * val	ex * pir * a * tion

Day 2

Do-now
Chapter 6:
R-control combination prompts #1

R-control combination prompts #1

Two or three R-control combinations can be added to each of these words. The parentheses after each word indicate the number of words to be made. Write the combinations that can be added to complete the words and write each word.

Prompts

p __ t (2)	f __ ce (2)	c __ t (2)
st __ (2)	f __ (3)	sp __ (2)
d __ t (2)	b __ n (2)	f __ m (3)
conf __ m (2)		

Answers

port/part	force/farce	cart/curt
star/stir	for/fir/fur	spar/spur
dirt/dart	burn/barn	firm/farm/form
confirm/conform		

Mini-lesson

Continue from Day 1.

Day 3

Do-now

Chapter 6:
R-control combination prompts #2

R-control combination prompts #2

Complete each word with one or two R-control combinations.

1. c ___ pent ___	1. carpenter
2. depl __ able	2. deplorable
3. abs __ bent	3. absorbent
4. m __ ble	4. marble
5. g __ den	5. garden
6. h __ tle	6. hurtle
7. resp __ ation	7. respiration
8. hamb __ g __	8. hamburger
9. cov ___ age	9. coverage
10. ch __ act __	10. character

Guided Practice

Chapter 6: Vocabulary graphic organizer
Chapter 6: "Sportsmanship" story

- **Time:** Fifteen minutes on one day.
- **Goal:** To expand reading vocabulary to contain R-control vowel combinations.
- **Materials:** Vocabulary graphic organizer, "Sportsmanship" story.
- **Overview:** Students read a passage with R-control vocabulary words and define them.

Directions

Read the words in the left column. Decide if you know the word, have heard or seen the word but are unsure of the meaning, or don't know the word at all. Mark the appropriate column. Determine the number of syllables in the word and list that number in the column. In the next column list the R-control vowel.

With a partner read the story "Sportsmanship." In the final column write the definition in your own words.

Vocabulary graphic organizer

Word	I know it	I've seen it or heard it, but am still unsure of the meaning	I don't know it!	Number of syllables	R-control vowel	Definition in my own words
irk						
sportsmanship						
smirk						
skirmish						
cornered						
shirk						
forlorn						
remorse						
deportment						
torrent						
minor						
deplorable						
defender						
embarrass						
distort						

"Sportsmanship" story

Sportsmanship

Last week we had a <u>soccer</u> game after school. One of the <u>defenders</u> on the <u>other</u> team and I had a <u>minor</u> <u>skirmish</u> because I thought I saw him <u>smirk</u> as I missed a shot at the goal. I spoke calmly to him about how he acted, but he showed no <u>remorse</u>. That really <u>irked</u> me. So I let loose on him with a <u>torrent</u> of <u>angry</u> remarks. I didn't know it at the time, but my English <u>instructor</u>, who is also my <u>soccer</u> coach, called my dad and told him that my <u>deportment</u> was not acceptable.

When I got home, my dad <u>cornered</u> me, yelled at me, and grounded me for a week. I was <u>forlorn</u>. It didn't seem right. I mean I explained what the <u>defender</u> on the <u>other</u> team had done to make me so <u>angry</u>, but my dad said I was <u>distorting</u> the facts. He explained that the coach had told him the whole <u>story</u> and that I was <u>trying</u> to <u>shirk</u> responsibility for my actions. He went on to say that my <u>behavior</u> was <u>embarrassing</u> and <u>deplorable</u>. I responded by saying I was sticking to my <u>story</u> and that I didn't feel badly because I was right. He asked me if I knew what <u>remorse</u> meant. I said, "Ya, I do, and that kid showed no <u>remorse</u> at all for laughing at me."

He grounded me for another week and told me to figure out what being <u>remorseful</u> had to do with me. I don't get parents.

Game—Pyramid Game Chapter 6: Pyramid

- **Time:** Fifteen minutes on one day.
- **Goal:** To identify the words that contain R-control vowels and syllables.
- **Materials:** Pyramid, timer.
- **Overview:** Display the pyramid so that only half the group can see it. Four to twenty students are divided into pairs, and one student gives examples of a category as the other attempts to guess the category.
- **Objective:** To guess the category.

Directions

1. Divide the class into pairs.
2. Player one sits with his back to the screen where the teacher has displayed the pyramid.
3. Player two faces her partner and the screen.
4. After the teacher says "start," player two begins at the bottom row of the pyramid naming words to fit the categories on the blocks one at a time without actually saying the category.
5. Player one attempts to guess the pyramid category his partner is describing.
6. Once he guesses a category, player two moves on to the next category.
7. The first pair to identify all of the categories on the pyramid is the winner.
8. If desired the teacher can set a timer for ten minutes and the winner is the pair with the most guessed categories at the end of the time period.

Pyramid

Three-syllable
IR

One-syllable OR
with W

One-syllable AR
with W

Two-syllable ER

Two-syllable AR

Two-syllable
UR

One-syllable
OR

One-syllable
IR

One-syllable ER

One-syllable
AR

Day 4

Do-now

Chapter 6:
R-control fill-in-the-blanks

R-control fill-in-the-blanks

Complete each sentence with a word from the word bank, and divide each of the words into syllables.

1. The _____ indicated that he would be able to transplant the _____.

2. At the _____ I rode on the _____ coaster.

3. I went to the _____ store to _____ a new _____.

4. During the race he jumped the _____ and won _____ place.

5. The _____ planted _____ in the field while his wife planted _____ in the _____.

carnival	doctor	organ
roller	department	purchase
purse	hurdles	first
farmer	corn	strawberries
garden		

Answers

1. The ___doc * tor___ indicated that he would be able to transplant the <u>or * gan</u> ___.
2. At the ___car * ni * val___ I rode on the ___roll * er___ coaster.
3. I went to the ___de * part * ment___ store to ___pur * chase___ a new ___purse___.
4. During the race he jumped the ___hur * dles___ and won ___first___ place.
5. The ___farm * er___ planted <u>corn</u> in the field while his wife planted <u>straw * ber * ries</u> in the ___gar * den___.

Independent Practice

Chapter 6:
R-control vowel worksheet #1

- **Time:** Fifteen minutes on one day.
- **Goal:** To identify the R-control vowel combination that will correctly complete a given word.
- **Materials:** R-control vowel worksheet #1.
- **Overview:** Individually, students identify the correct R-control vowel combination to complete a word.

R-control vowel worksheet #1

Directions

Fill in the missing R-control vowel combinations ("ir," "er," "ur," "or," "ar")

c _ _ ton	b_ _thday	ch_ _ p	p_ _ch
c _ _ tain	ch_ _m	f _ _ ce	us _ _
transp_ _t	st _ _ m	st _ _ light	p _ _ k
m_ _ ning	anoth _ _	doct _ _	c _ _ l
carpent_ _	ch _ _ ish	p _ _ cussion	chapt _ _
b_ _ n	th_ _ n	c_ _ pet	fing_ _
f _ _ nish	plast_ _	_ _ gan	c_ _ nival
f_ _ m_ _	w _ _	w _ _ m	w _ _ d
awkw_ _ d	w_ _ ship	t_ _ tle	d_ _mant
b_ _ t_ _	g _ _ ble	c _ _ dinal	h_ _dle
f_ _ mat	c_ _ dboard	met_ _	fold_ _
mot_ _	crat_ _	bak _ _	comput _ _

Using the previous words and any additional words, write twelve words in each column.

AR	ER	IR	OR	UR

Answers

c <u>a r</u> ton   b <u>i r</u> thday   ch <u>i r</u> p   p <u>o r</u> ch or p <u>e r</u> ch

c <u>u r</u> tain   ch <u>a r</u> m   f <u>o r</u> ce   us <u>e r</u>

transp <u>o r</u> t   st <u>o r</u> m   st <u>a r</u> light   p <u>a r</u> k or p <u>o r</u> k

m <u>o r</u> ning   anoth <u>e r</u>   doct <u>o r</u>   c <u>u r</u> l

carpent <u>e r</u>   ch <u>e r</u> ish   p <u>e r</u> cussion   chapt <u>e r</u>

b <u>a r</u> n or b <u>u r</u> n   th <u>o r</u> n   c <u>a r</u> pet   fing <u>e r</u>

f <u>u r</u> nish   plast <u>e r</u>   <u>o r</u> gan   c <u>a r</u> nival

f <u>a r</u> m <u>e r</u>   w <u>a r</u>   w <u>o r</u> m   w <u>o r</u> d

awkw <u>a r</u> d   w <u>o r</u> ship   t <u>u r</u> tle   d <u>o r</u> mant

b <u>a r</u> t <u>e r</u>   g <u>a r</u> ble   c <u>a r</u> dinal   h <u>u r</u> dle

f <u>o r</u> mat   c <u>a r</u> dboard   met <u>e r</u>   fold <u>e r</u>

mot <u>o r</u>   crat <u>e r</u>   bak <u>e r</u>   comput <u>e r</u>

AR	ER	IR	OR	UR
card	crater	dirt	motor	hurt
cardboard	baker	skirt	dormant	furnish
cardinal	meter	shirt	word	burn
carnival	computer	flirt	worm	turtle
star	finger	firm	thorn	hurdle
park	farmer	bird	born	curtain
carpenter	barter	sir	organ	gurgle
carve	plaster	stir	porch	burglar
awkward	teacher	birthday	format	turn
carton	bigger	girl	pork	churn
ward	perch	third	worship	absurd
charm	another	birth	doctor	church

- **Time:** Fifteen minutes on one day.
- **Goal:** To identify the R-control vowel combination that will correctly complete a given word and to use the words in sentences.
- **Materials:** R-control vowel worksheet #2.
- **Overview:** Individually, students identify the correct R-control vowel combination to complete a word and then use it in a sentence.

R-control vowel worksheet #2

Directions

Complete each one syllable word by adding "ar," "er," "ir," "or," or "ur" in the blanks.

ch_ _m	f _ _ ce	ch_ _ p	p_ _ch
p _ _ k	c _ _ l	b_ _ n	th_ _ n
st _ _ m	sp _ _ k	c _ _ d	ch _ _ n
w _ _	w _ _ m	w _ _ d	wh _ _ f

Complete each two- or three-syllable word by adding "ar," "er," "ir," "or," or "ur."

m_ _ ning	anoth _ _	doct _ _	exp _ _ ation
us_ _	chapt_ _	mot_ _	crat_ _
f_ _ nish	plast_ _	_ _ gan	c _ _ nival
b_ _ t_ _	g _ _ ble	c_ _ dinal	h_ _dle
c _ _ cul _ _	conf _ _ m	sk _ _ mish	adm _ _ ation
c _ _ cle	c _ _ cumf _ _ ence	asp _ _ in	s _ _ loin
adm _ _ al	enc _ _ cle	v _ _ tual	persp _ _ ation

Use five of the two- or three-syllable words in sentences.

_____

_____

_____

_____

_____

_____

_____

_____

_____

Answers

ch **ar** m	f **or** ce	ch **ir** p	p **or** ch or p **er** ch
p **ar** k or p **or** k	c **ur** l	b **ar** n or b **ur** n	th **or** n
st **or** m	sp **ar** k	c **ar** d or c **or** d	ch **ur** n
w **ar**	w **ar** m or w **or** m	w **or** d or w **ar** d	wh **ar** f
m **or** ning	anoth **er**	doct **or**	exp **ir** ation
mor ning	an oth er	doc tor	ex pir a tion
us **er**	chapt **er**	mot **or**	crat **er**
u ser	chap ter	mo tor	cra ter
f **ur** nish	plast **er**	**or** gan	c **ar** nival
fur nish	plas ter	or gan	car ni val
b **ar** t **er**	g **ar** ble	c **ar** dinal	h **ur** dle
bar ter	gar ble	car din al	hur dle
c **ir** cul **ar**	conf **ir** m	sk **ir** mish	adm **ir** ation
cir cu lar	con firm	skir mish	ad mir a tion
c **ir** cle	c **ir** cumf **er** ence	asp **ir** in	s **ir** loin
cir cle	cir cum fer ence	as pir in	sir loin
adm **ir** al	enc **ir** cle	v **ir** tual	persp **ir** ation
ad mir al	en cir cle	vir tu al	per spir a tion

Answers will vary.

_____

_____

_____

_____

_____

_____

_____

Day 5

Do-now
Chapter 6:
Syllable matching list

Syllable matching list

Match a syllable on the left with a syllable on the right to form a word.

con	bid
for	tort
hor	firm
mor	er
warm	ect
wor	net
skir	ward
birth	ry
dir	mark
re	mish

Write the three words where the "w" changes the sound of the R-control vowel.

Answers

confirm, forward, hornet, morbid, warmer, worry, skirmish, birthmark, direct, retort

W impacting an R-control vowel—forward, warmer, worry

Post-test—R-control Syllables
Chapter 6:
Post-test—R-control syllables

Indicate how many syllables are in each word. If the word can be divided into syllables, indicate how it is divided.

Example: trispen   <u> 2   tris * pen </u>

1. spartle   _____

2. sircumstand   _____

3. inspirattle   _____

4. worgirant   _____

5. gerth   _____

6. blurter   _____

7. gymquirt   _____

8. uncontrester   _____

9. antrimpor   _____

10. yestpar   _____

Write the words that your teacher dictates for each question.

1. _____   6. _____
2. _____   7. _____
3. _____   8. _____
4. _____   9. _____
5. _____   10. _____

Read the following passage orally.

The <u>Farmer</u> and the <u>Sterm</u>

One <u>winter</u> a <u>farmer</u> found a <u>sterm</u> <u>starf</u> and <u>frozen</u> with <u>incord</u>. He had <u>darpressert</u> on it, and <u>taking</u> it up, placed it in his <u>bresserm</u>. The <u>sterm</u> was <u>quickly</u> <u>reverted</u> by the <u>warmth</u>, and <u>resumting</u> its natural instincts, bit its <u>bennefractor</u>, <u>inflicting</u> on him a <u>mortal</u> <u>wernd</u>. "Oh," cried the <u>Farmer</u> with his last <u>gerth</u>, "I am rightly <u>served</u> for <u>pretting</u> a <u>scurndrel</u>." The greatest kindness will not <u>burd</u> the <u>ungratful.</u>

Answers

1. sparle   <u>2   spar * tle</u>
2. sircumstand   <u>3   sir * cum * stand</u>
3. inspirattle   <u>4   in * spir * at * tle</u>
4. worgirant   <u>3   wor * gir * ant</u>
5. gerth   <u>1   gerth</u>
6. blurter   <u>2   blur * ter</u>
7. gymquirt   <u>2   gym * quirt</u>
8. uncontrester   <u>4   un * con * tres * ter</u>
9. antrimpor   <u>3   an * trim * por</u>
10. yestpar   <u>2   yest * par</u>

1. <u>   farn * der   </u>   6. <u>   trep * pen   </u>
2. <u>   con * ter * tle   </u> 7. <u>   drun * dar   </u>
3. <u>   bri * gle   </u>   8. <u>   grat * tle   </u>
4. <u>   cler * zle   </u>   9. <u>   sis * tar   </u>
5. <u>   yur * ble   </u>   10. <u>   flog * ger   </u>

The <u>Farm</u> * er and the <u>Sterm</u>

One <u>win * ter</u> a <u>farm * er</u> found a <u>sterm</u> <u>starf</u> and <u>fro * zen</u> with <u>in * cord</u>. He had <u>dar * pres * sert</u> on it, and <u>ta * king</u> it up, placed it in his <u>bres * serm</u>. The <u>sterm</u> was <u>quick * ly</u> <u>re * ver * ted</u> by the <u>warmth</u>, and <u>re * sum * ting</u> its natural <u>in * stincts</u>, bit its <u>ben * ne * frac * tor</u>, <u>in * flict * ing</u> on him a <u>mor * tal</u> <u>wernd</u>. "Oh," cried the <u>Farm * er</u> with his last <u>gerth</u>, "I am rightly served for <u>prêt * ting</u> a <u>scurn * drel</u>." The greatest kindness will not <u>burd</u> the <u>un * grat * ful</u>.

Scoring: Number of underlined words correct   /26

Chap·ter 7
CVCe Syllable

Sequence	Suggested Time Frame	Moving to Automaticity	Time	Materials
Week 6: CVCe	Day 1	Do-now	10 min.	CVCe vocabulary fill-in-the-blanks #1
	Day 1	Mini-lesson	10 min.	Classroom white board, example words
	Day 2	Do-now	10 min.	CVCe vocabulary fill-in-the-blanks #2
	Day 2	Guided Practice	15 min.	Classroom white board, notebook paper
	Day 3	Do-now	10 min.	CVCe vocabulary fill-in-the-blanks #3
	Day 3	Game—Rolling Along	15 min.	Rolling Along word cards
	Day 4	Do-now	10 min.	CVCe vocabulary fill-in-the-blanks #4
	Day 4	Game—Rolling Along	15 min.	Rolling Along word cards
	Day 5	Do-now	10 min.	CVCe vocabulary fill-in-the-blanks #5
	Day 5	Independent Practice	15 min.	Cloze extension worksheet #1
Week 7: Two-syllable CVCe	Day 1	Do-now	10 min.	CVCe vocabulary fill-in-the-blanks #6
	Day 1	Mini-lesson	15 min.	Classroom white boards
	Day 2	Do-now	10 min.	CVCe vocabulary fill-in-the-blanks #7
	Day 2	Guided Practice	15 min.	Blend graphic organizer, digraph graphic organizer, CVCe word list
	Day 2 or 3	Game—Star-spangled Path	15 min.	Star-spangled cards, Star-spangled game board, dice
	Day 3	Do-now	10 min.	CVCe vocabulary fill-in-the-blanks #8
	Day 3	Independent Practice	15 min.	Cloze extension worksheet #2
	Day 4	Do-now	10 min.	CVCe vocabulary fill-in-the-blanks #9
	Day 4	Extension	15 min.	Multisyllabic CVCe word list
	Day 5	Do-now	10 min.	CVCe vocabulary fill-in-the-blanks #10
	Day 5	Post-test	20 min.	Post-test—CVCe

Week 6

Day 1

Do-nows
Chapter 7:
CVCe vocabulary fill-in-the-blanks #1

CVCe vocabulary fill-in-the-blanks #1

Read the numbered words and their definitions. Determine the word to be used in each sentence.

It was my sixteenth birthday and I had spent the past month planning the best party I have ever or would ever have. On the morning of my party, my best friend Maggie planned to come over early to help me decorate. I had placed the decorations on the table the night before and felt completely ready for her arrival early that morning. I woke up in a great mood ready to have the best day of my life and went straight to the kitchen for some breakfast. Passing though the dining room, I almost fainted. My party supplies were strewn all over the dining room and most of the paper products were in shreds. I was very upset, but I tried to _____ myself and since no one was up to scream at, I went to lie on my bed for a minute. While lying in _____, I tried to think who would have done such a thing. I could only think of one person, my little brother, Andrew. He was always destroying things, especially things that belonged to me. His nickname was aptly Hurricane Andrew. I would have to _____ a confession from him before killing him, but that was only a formality. I would make him pay before the day was over.

1. repose: (v) to lie at rest; to put back; to put away; (n) peace, tranquility, calm
2. compose: (v) to put together; to arrange; to bring oneself to a condition of calmness, repose
3. depose: (v) to remove from office; to testify under oath; to state or affirm in a deposition

Answers
1. compose
2. repose
3. depose

Mini-lesson
- **Time:** Ten minutes on one day.
- **Goal:** To develop proficiency encoding words with CVCe syllables.
- **Materials:** Classroom white board, example words.
- **Overview:** Students determine the effect the final e has on the vowel sound in the CVCe syllable.

Directions

Students have now covered four types of syllables: CVC, CV, Cle, and R-control. Review with students the difference between the long and short vowel sounds. Also remind students that approximately 84 percent of English words are phonetically regular. Therefore, teaching the most common sound-spelling relationships in English is extremely useful for readers. As Anderson et al. (1985) write, "English is an alphabetic language in which there are consistent, though not entirely predictable, relationships between letters and sounds." Students need to develop proficiency in identifying the relationship between letters and sounds so that most of the words in their spoken vocabulary become accessible to them in the printed form.

Students should be reminded that every syllable has one vowel sound. If a word or syllable is a CVC syllable, then the vowel in that syllable is generally short. If the word or syllable is CV, then the vowel is generally long. However, there is also a CVCe syllable. This syllable is only found at the end of a single syllable or multisyllabic word.

This is a simple phonics rule that most students learned in the primary grades; however, some students may benefit from reteaching of this rule. Demonstrate the effect of the silent "e" by writing the words below on the board. Have students identify the difference between the two words and recall the rule. Students will notice that when an "e" is added as the last letter of the word, it changes the vowel sound from short to long.

| hat | pet | hid | hop | cub |
| hate | Pete | hide | hope | cube |

Day 2

Do-now

Chapter 7:
CVCe vocabulary fill-in-the-blanks #2

CVCe vocabulary fill-in-the-blanks #2

I suppose his _____ was to destroy my party and pay me back for getting him grounded last week for stealing my cell phone, but he can't _____with me when it comes to pay back. I planned on getting him good.

Although I didn't want to _____ on Maggie, I called her to see if she could come over even earlier to help me figure out how to salvage my party supplies and pay back my little monster of a brother.

1. purpose: (n) an aim or a goal; the matter at hand
2. impose: (v) to lay or inflict as a penalty; to take unfair advantage of; to misuse
3. compete: (v) to try to beat others in a contest, fight, etc.

Answers

1. purpose
2. compete
3. impose

Maggie arrived thirty minutes after my phone call with all sorts of supplies to _____ to the party decorations. This was the _____ that made me appreciate Maggie the most, her generosity. She was generous with all her stuff and most especially her time. It didn't take us long to _____ what we needed to do, and we got to work turning the family room and backyard into a tropical island.

1. attribute: (v) to relate to a particular cause or source; (n) a quality or characteristic inherent in or ascribed to someone or something
2. contribute: (v) to give (money, time, food, knowledge, assistance, etc.)
3. decide: (v) to solve or conclude; to determine or settle

Answers
1. contribute
2. attribute
3. decide

Guided Practice

- **Time:** Fifteen minutes on one day.
- **Goal:** To combine syllables with CVCe syllables to form additional words.
- **Materials:** Classroom white board, notebook paper.
- **Overview:** Students will combine additional syllables with specified CVCe syllables.

Directions

Write the root word "pute" on the board. Explain to students that additional syllables can be added to "pute" to form different words. Ask the students if they are able to think of a syllable that can be added to form a word. If necessary, prompt them with the syllable "dis." On the board write the word "dispute." Additional words that can be formed include compute, repute, and computer.

Working in pairs, students will form words from the following syllables: "pose," "cline," and "tude." The pair that forms the most words wins.

Day 3

Do-now
Chapter 7:
CVCe vocabulary fill-in-the-blanks #3

CVCe vocabulary fill-in-the-blanks #3

In an effort to _____ the good mood I started the day with, Maggie and I went out for an early lunch. We came back with the intention of resting a bit before we got dressed for the party. When I walked into the family room, I literally screamed out loud. The party decorations were all over the floor and half of them in shreds. I was close to hysterical. Maggie tried to calm me down and instructed me in deep breathing.

She told me to draw my breath in slowly and let it out slowly. She continued to coach me with, "_____, take your breath in calmly, and _____ let your breath out slowly." It worked; I felt calmer, but boy was I angry.

1. exhale: (v) to emit breath or vapor; to breathe out
2. inhale: (v) to draw in by breathing
3. reprise: (n) an annual deduction, duty, or payment out of a manor or estate; (v) to execute a repetition of; to repeat

Answers

1. reprise
2. inhale
3. exhale

Game—Rolling Along

Chapter 7:
Rolling Along word cards

Note: You can play this game on both Days 3 and 4.
- **Time:** Fifteen minutes per day; play game twice.
- **Goal:** To match CVC and CVCe words whose only difference is the final "e."
- **Materials:** Rolling Along word cards.
- **Overview:** Players turn over two cards to find CVC and CVCe words that are the same except for the final "e."
- **Objective:** To get more matches than the other players.

Directions

1. Dealer shuffles the cards and then spreads them out on the table with the words face down.
2. The first player turns over two cards and reads the word on each card.
3. If the player turns over two cards whose only difference is the final silent "e," the cards are a match.
4. If the player reads the words correctly, she takes the match and takes another turn.
5. If the player does not read the cards correctly or if they do not match, the cards are turned back over and placed in the same position on the table.
6. Then it is the next person's turn.
7. Play continues until all the cards are gone.
8. The person with the most matches wins.

Answers

plan-plane	spin-spine	bit-bite
can-cane	dim-dime	prim-prime
rid-ride	fin-fine	cap-cape
hop-hope	kit-kite	cub-cube
cop-cope	pin-pine	man-mane
rat-rate	slop-slope	past-paste
plum-plume	rip-ripe	strip-stripe
shin-shine	writ-write	rob-robe
tub-tube	hat-hate	ban-bane
spit-spite	mop-mope	hid-hide

Do-now Chapter 7:
CVCe vocabulary fill-in-the-blanks #4

CVCe vocabulary fill-in-the-blanks #4

It was now definite. That _____ of a brother I had was doomed. He thought he was emperor of this kingdom, but I was about to bring his _____ down around his ears! I'm usually not one to _____ against another individual, but seriously, Hurricane Andrew had it coming. While we were plotting his demise, my mother bounded into the room. The look on her face as she scanned the destruction was shock. "Rachel! What happened?" she gasped.

1. reprobate: (n) a depraved, unprincipled, or wicked person; (adj) morally depraved; unprincipled, bad
2. conspire: (v) to plot (something wrong, evil or illegal); to act or work together toward the same goal
3. empire: (n) a group of nations or peoples ruled over by an emperor, empress, or other powerful sovereign or government

Answers

1. reprobate
2. empire
3. conspire

You have to _____ my mom. She never looks at a situation and says, "What happened?" without saying, "What can I do?" I'm not certain I'll ever _____ that kind of attitude, but I _____ to be like her.

1. admire: (v) to regard with wonder, pleasure, or approval
2. acquire: (v) to gain possession of; to gain through experience; to come by
3. aspire: (v) to long, aim, or seek ambitiously; to be eagerly desirous, especially for something great or of high value

Answers

1. admire
2. acquire
3. aspire

Game—Rolling Along

Continue from Day 3.

Day 5

Do-now Chapter 7:
CVCe vocabulary fill-in-the-blanks #5

CVCe vocabulary fill-in-the-blanks #5

I can honestly say that my mother would never _____ me of anything she could give me. She has given me everything I need, and even some things that I don't. She has been a single mom since I was twelve and my brother was six, but she has always worked to _____us with all that we needed and more. There is nothing I would do to _____ my mother. She doesn't need to be better. She is perfect just the way she is. I keep telling her that, but she still doesn't realize it.

1. deprive: (v) to remove or withhold something from the enjoyment or possession of
2. refine: (v) to become more fine, elegant, or polished; to bring to a fine or a pure state; to free from impurities
3. provide: (v) to furnish; supply; to make available

Answers

1. deprive
2. provide
3. refine

Independent Practice Chapter 7:
Cloze extension worksheet #1

- **Time:** Fifteen minutes for one day.
- **Goal:** To use in context words that are the same except for the final "e."
- **Materials:** Cloze extension worksheet #1.
- **Overview:** Working with a partner, students identify words that will make sense in each sentence.

Cloze extension worksheet #1
Directions

Work with a partner to complete the Cloze Extension sheet. The only difference between the two words used in the blanks in each sentence is one has the silent "e" and one does not.

1. The aeronautical engineer came up with a _____ to market his new commercial _____ in the United States.

2. After the 4th of July concert, the blind woman walked carefully through the trash-strewn park, accidentally slipping as her _____ became lodged in a carelessly discarded soda _____.

3. The mechanical engineer worked after park hours to try to _____ the new roller coaster _____ of stalls on the second loop.

4. The rabbit took one last, frantic _____ toward the fence with the _____ of escaping the relentless fox that was chasing him.

5. Everyone in the cooperative group helped as they had promised except for one _____-out with whom they tried to _____.

6. The heartbeat of the lab _____ increased at a steady _____ as he ran effortlessly on the exercise wheel in his laboratory cage.

7. The soft, fluffy _____ of the heron was a deep purple color that resembled the fruit of the _____ tree.

8. In preparation for my dance performance, I put lotion on the _____ of my leg to make it noticeably _____ as I tapped out my routine.

9. I squeezed the _____ of bath bubbles into the _____ before I ran the water.

10. I tried to _____ the gum from my mouth into the trash can in _____ of the fact that the teacher told me I was getting a detention for chewing it in class again today.

11. I placed the library book on its _____ and tried to _____it a full 360 degrees on the table.

12. The light in the room was so _____ that I could not see if I had a _____ or a penny in my hand.

13. Linda grabbed the fish from the net and the _____, slender _____ of the captured fish sliced her finger.

14. We purchased a _____ to make a _____ of our own design for flying on windy days in the park.

15. The sharp needle from the _____ tree felt like a sharp _____as it stuck in the tip of my finger.

Answers

1. plan, plane
2. cane, can
3. rid, ride
4. hop, hope
5. cop, cope
6. rat, rate
7. plume, plum
8. shin, shine
9. tube, tub
10. spit, spite
11. spine, spin
12. dim, dime
13. fine, fin
14. kit, kite
15. pine, pin

Week 7

Day 1

Do-now Chapter 7:
CVCe vocabulary fill-in-the-blanks #6

CVCe vocabulary fill-in-the-blanks #6

"It was Andrew," I screamed. "He is trying to ruin my party! This is so typical of him!"
Mom calmly answered, "Andrew would never do this intentionally. I'm sorry this has happened, but you can't blame your brother." She then rushed from the room calling Andrew's name.

Maggie asked if my mom could be right. She said she didn't think even Hurricane Andrew would be so mean to _____ such a plan to destroy my party. I informed her that this would not be the first time he tried to _____ with his friends to make my life miserable, and that I was sure he was the culprit. Maggie tried to _____ with me whether or not Andrew was capable of such evil, but in my opinion there was no question: Andrew was guilty!

1. contrive: (v) to plan with ingenuity; to devise; to invent
2. connive: (v) to cooperate secretly; to conspire
3. debate: (n) a discussion, as of a public question in an assembly, involving opposing viewpoints; (v) to engage in argument or discussion

Answers

1. contrive
2. connive
3. debate

Mini-lesson

- **Time:** Fifteen minutes on one day.
- **Goal:** To identify how consonant digraphs affect syllable division.
- **Materials:** Classroom white boards.
- **Overview:** Students divide words containing consonant digraphs into syllables.

Directions

In Chapter 3 students learned some of the basic rules of syllabication to help them determine the correct vowel sound in a syllable. Creating an understanding that some letters blend together and others combine to form a new sound is necessary for the correct division of multisyllabic words.

In Chapter 4 students were taught to first underline the vowels in the word to determine how many syllables there were. If they found two vowel sounds, they were to count the number of consonants between the sounds. If between the underlined vowels there were two consonants, they were to divide the word into syllables between the two consonants. However, in words like conspire, the "sp" blend remains together to form the onset of the second syllable.

In the word "conspire" the first step would be to underline the vowels: conspire. Step two would be to count the consonants between the vowels. Between the underlined vowels there are actually three consonants: "nsp." Since "sp" is a consonant blend, the word would be divided between the "n" and the "s": con * spire. Based on their understanding of the CVC and CVCe syllables, students will recognize that the vowel sound in the first syllable is short and the vowel sound in the second syllable is long.

Day 2

Do-now 💿 Chapter 7:
CVCe vocabulary fill-in-the-blanks #7

CVCe vocabulary fill-in-the-blanks #7

With _____d efforts Maggie and I managed to put together a pretty cool party ambiance, and ultimately I knew that my friends would _____ my party as the best one of the year. Although we had to _____ ourselves to the family room and backyard, it really did have the atmosphere of a tropical island.

1. combine: (v) to bring into or join in a close union or whole; to unite; (n) a harvesting machine for cutting and threshing grain in the field
2. define: (v) to explain or identify the nature or essential qualities of; to describe; to state or set forth the meaning of (a word, phrase, etc.)
3. confine: (n) usually, confines; a boundary or bound; limit; border; frontier; (v) to enclose within bounds; to limit or restrict

Answers

1. combine
2. define
3. confine

At 8:00 sharp the doorbell rang, and my first guest arrived dressed in a tropical shirt and carrying the _____d invitation. Soon the yard and house were filled with people wearing leis and wildly printed clothes. Enough food and drink was _____d to feed a small country, and we danced and sang karaoke. Despite all of the trouble getting ready for it, it was a pretty great party. At about midnight, everyone was encouraging me to open my gifts, which I hadn't planned on actually doing at the party, but my friends begged me to do it so I did. Maggie kept a list of who gave me what and my friend Bethany, who was a perfectionist, immediately _____d it into a new and more neatly written copy for me to refer to later. (I have great friends.) I loved everything, even the stupid gag gifts. It was the best party ever!

1. inscribe: (v) to write, print, or engrave words or letters on a surface
2. transcribe: (v) to write out an exact copy of something; to translate something
3. consume: (v) to eat or drink something, especially in large amounts

Answers

1. inscribe
2. consume
3. transcribe

Guided Practice

Chapter 7: Blend graphic organizer
Chapter 7: Digraph graphic organizer
Chapter 7: CVCe word list

- **Time:** Fifteen minutes on one day.
- **Goal:** To understand how blends and digraphs affect syllable division.
- **Materials:** Blend graphic organizer, digraph graphic organizer, CVCe word list.
- **Overview:** Pairs of two to twenty students complete a graphic organizer of blend and digraphs and use this understanding to divide words into syllables.

Directions

Explain to students that a blend is two or more consonants that run together or blend. They can hear the sound of each of the consonants in a blend. Working in pairs, students brainstorm as many words as they can containing blends or digraphs to complete the following chart.

Blend graphic organizer

bl	cl	gl	fl	pl
sl	br	cr	dr	fr
gr	pr	tr	sc	sk
sm	sn	sp	st	sw
scr	str	spl	spr	thr

Explain that a consonant digraph is the combination of two consonant sounds to make a new sound. Remind students that the blend or digraph is not always at the beginning of a word. Blends and digraphs can often be found at the end of a word, as in "defend" and "punch," or in the middle of a word, as in "longest" and "whiskers." The blend or digraph tends to be treated as one consonant sound and is usually placed in the same syllable, rather than divided between two different syllables.

As a class, brainstorm multiple words for each of the following consonant digraphs.

Digraph graphic organizer

ch	sh	th	wh	ph	qu

Remind students, as we learned in Chapter 4, that if they discover there is just one consonant or one consonant blend between the two vowels, they should divide before the consonant or before the consonant blend. The initial syllable would then have a long vowel sound. If this does not produce a word that they recognize, they should then try dividing the word after the consonant, making the first vowel sound short. Model dividing the first three words in the list below into syllables. Have students work in pairs to divide the remaining words into syllables. After they have divided the words, the students should practice pronouncing the words correctly.

CVCe word list

1. repose
2. compose
3. depose
4. purpose
5. impose
6. compete
7. attribute
8. contribute
9. decide
10. exhale
11. inhale
12. reprise
13. reprobate
14. conspire
15. empire

Game—Star-spangled Path

Chapter 7: Star-spangled cards
Chapter 7: Star-spangled game board

Note: You can do this exercise on either Day 2 or 3.
- **Time:** Fifteen minutes on one day.
- **Goal:** To read CVCe words correctly.
- **Materials:** Star-spangled cards, Star-spangled game board, dice.
- **Overview:** Students move around the board by rolling dice and reading the word on the card correctly.
- **Objective:** To reach the finish line before the other players.

Directions

1. The star spangled cards are shuffled and placed face down in a single pile on the table next to the playing board.
2. Each player rolls the dice to see who gets the lowest number. The player with the lowest number goes first.
3. The first player turns over the first card in the pile and reads the word on the card.

4. If the player reads the word correctly, she rolls the dice and moves that many spaces on the board.

5. If the player lands on a circle with printed directions, she follows the directions.

6. If the player lands on a circle with an arrow, he follows the arrow to the new circle. Then his turn ends.

7. The next player proceeds in the same manner by reading the word and then rolling the dice.

8. The first player to reach the finish line is the winner.

9. As students become proficient reading the words, the game moves to a harder level. This time the player must appropriately use the word in a sentence. The sentence must demonstrate that the individual understands the meaning of the word.

10. When playing this game using sentences, it might be easier to play as teams. This format allows the students to work together to compose appropriate sentences.

Day 3

Do-now Chapter 7: CVCe vocabulary fill-in-the-blanks #8

CVCe vocabulary fill-in-the-blanks #8

Just when I was feeling absolutely _____, Hurricane Andrew came barreling into the party. I could tell he was mad. You see, before the party started Maggie and I worked together to basically trash his room. We slathered the door handle with Vaseline and short-sheeted his bed, but that wasn't what he was mad about. I took his game system and (okay, I admit I may have gone a bit far here) I broke all of the strings on his guitar. We got onto his computer and changed his away message to, "I am just a dumb little ten-year-old who will never have a girlfriend because I won't be able to stand being around anyone prettier than I am. I'm away right now playing Barbies at my friend's house."

He was mad, and tried to get me to admit what I had done. I _____d to admit guilt. My mom tried to _____ the situation by telling Andrew that we would discuss it after the party was over. People were starting to leave, but Mom announced that there was one more big surprise that Andrew had for me, and asked everyone to stay a few more minutes.

1. sublime: (n) the greatest or supreme degree; (v) to make higher, nobler, or purer; (adj) supreme or outstanding
2. refuse: (n) something that is discarded as worthless or useless; rubbish; trash; garbage; (v) to decline to accept
3. defuse: (v) to remove the fuse from (an explosive device); to make less dangerous, tense, or hostile

Answers

1. sublime
2. refuse
3. defuse

Independent Practice

- **Time:** Fifteen minutes on one day.
- **Goal:** To use CVC and CVCe words to complete sentences.
- **Materials:** Cloze extension worksheet #2.
- **Overview:** Working in pairs, students complete sentences with CVC and CVCe words.

Cloze extension worksheet #2
Directions

Work with a partner to complete the cloze extension worksheet. The only difference between the two words used in the blanks in each sentence is that one has the silent "e" and one does not.

1. As the pig walked up the steep _____, he slid into the _____ that was his dinner.

2. I tried to _____ the _____, juicy orange from the fruit tree in our back yard, but it would have been more effective to pluck it!

3. The Parliament of England was asked by the Queen to _____ a formal _____ declaring a day of mourning for the passing of their King.

4. It was winter and despite how it made me _____ my hair, I decided to wear a _____ to keep my head warm.

5. When helping my mom clean the house last week, I wanted to _____ the floor, but that job went to my sister Rachel, and I had to clean the bathrooms. Mom yelled at me and told me not to _____ about it because I would get to choose my job first next week.

6. When I was holding my baby sister, she _____ my arm and left teeth marks! I wanted to _____ her back, but I knew better. She was, after all, just a baby and didn't mean to hurt me.

7. The restaurant was so fancy that the very _____ and proper waiter, placed my cloth napkin on my lap before serving me my _____ rib entrée.

8. In our school theatrical production, I played Amy from *Little Women*. It was supposed to be wintertime so I donned a black, velvet _____ and wore a matching _____ over my shoulders.

9. The bear's baby _____ sat in a _____-shaped cage at the city zoo.

10. We watched in awe as the _____ who was the first act in the trick-riding show grabbed the racing horse's _____ and swung his legs over the horse's back.

11. In the _____, when I was young, we licked stamps to _____ them on an envelope. Today, stamps are self-sticking and wetting the back is no longer necessary.

12. To paint a _____ on my living room wall, I used a _____ of tape on the area I did not want painted.

13. The infamous thief was known as "Sleepy Robin Hood" because he would _____ from the rich while wearing a bath_____ and immediately drop the money he had stolen at various charitable organizations throughout the city.

14. We tried to _____ all fattening foods from our house because over-eating was the _____ of our dad's existence.

15. When we played _____ n' Seek with our younger cousins, I _____ in the closet in my bedroom every time and yet they never found me.

Answers

1. slope, slop
2. rip, ripe
3. write, writ
4. hate, hat
5. mop, mope
6. bit, bite
7. prim, prime
8. cap, cape
9. cub, cube
10. man, mane
15. past, paste
12. stripe, strip
13. rob, robe
14. ban, bane
15. hide, hid

Day 4

Do-now   Chapter 7:
CVCe vocabulary fill-in-the-blanks #9

CVCe vocabulary fill-in-the-blanks #9

I looked over at Andrew and he was looking mad and upset in the corner of the room. I could only _____ that Andrew's big surprise was one more attempt at ruining my party, but my mom would not take part in that and she seemed to know what was going on. I admit I was _____d. It is difficult for me to _____ how I felt after what happened next. Andrew slowly rose and left the family room for a minute. When he came back he was carrying a great big box with a huge pink bow on top.

1. confuse: (v) to perplex or bewilder; to fail to distinguish between; to associate by mistake; to confound
2. describe: (v) to tell or depict in written or spoken words; to give an account of
3. assume: (v) to take upon oneself; undertake; to take for granted or without proof; to suppose; to postulate

Answers

1. assume
2. confused
3. describe

Extension   Chapter 7:
Multisyllabic CVCe word list

- **Time:** Fifteen minutes on one day.
- **Goal:** To divide the multisyllabic CVCe words into syllables and use them in context.
- **Overview:** Individually, students divide the words into syllables and then use them in a story.
- **Materials:** Multisyllabic CVCe word list.

Multisyllabic CVCe word list

Directions
Independently divide the following words into syllables. Then use at least six of the words in a story. Be prepared to read your story to the class.

1. admire	2. acquire	3. aspire
4. deprive	5. refine	6. provide
7. contrive	8. connive	9. debate
10. combine	11. define	12. confine
13. inscribe	14. transcribe	15. consume
16. sublime	17. refuse	18. defuse
19. confuse	20. circumscribe	21. assume
22. respite	23. contrite	24. stipulate

Answers

1. ad * mire	2. ac * quire	3. as * pire
4. de * prive	5. re * fine	6. pro * vide
7. con * trive	8. con * nive	9. de * bate
10. com * bine	11. de * fine	12. con * fine
13. in * scribe	14. tran * scribe	15. con * sume
16. sub * lime	17. re * fuse	18. de * fuse
19. con * fuse	20. cir * cum * scribe	21. as * sume
22. re * spite	23. con * trite	24. stip * u * late

Day 5

Do-now Chapter 7:
CVCe vocabulary fill-in-the-blanks #10

CVCe vocabulary fill-in-the-blanks #10

Andrew walked slowly toward me wearing a slight smile. The large box he held began to erupt and he carefully set it on the floor at my feet. I tentatively reached to lift the lid, afraid that I was about to be blasted with some sort of spewing liquid when the lid lifted itself and almost immediately a furry, warm animal burst forth and leaped onto my lap. It was a Golden Retriever pup—beautiful and soft and wildly squirmy! Tears began to flow from my eyes. I had wanted a Golden Retriever since I was a baby myself. I looked first at Andrew and then at my mom. Mom was crying and explained, "Andrew has been saving for more than a year to buy you that puppy. He tried to keep it a surprise, but it was almost ruined when the feisty little pup got loose and tore apart your party supplies. I'm surprised you weren't suspicious!"

I can't describe the _____ feeling I had at that moment. My little brother, my nemesis, had just given me the best gift I have ever received, and, I'm sure, that I will ever receive. My little Hurricane Andrew, whom I had treated so badly...I began to sob with guilt and happiness all at once. I rose, hugged my little brother, apologizing and thanking him at the same time.

Feeling drained, I stood at the door thanking my guests while the little pup ripped through the family room, attacking gift wrap and packages with a mischievous vengeance.
Andrew tried to contain him but it was no use...the little guy was like a tornado, destroying everything in his path.

After everyone was gone, I sat with my mom and Andrew playing with my new puppy. My mom spoke softly but firmly. "Well, Rachel, this was some birthday. I'm going to offer you a period of _____ before you make amends for the destruction you brought upon Andrew today, and I am going to _____ that if you want to keep this puppy, you must promise me that from now on, before blaming your brother for everything that goes wrong in your day, you will think of this wonderful and loving gesture first, and remember how wrong you were about his intentions."

I nodded and looked tearfully at Andrew. I quietly choked out, "I am so sorry, Andrew." I guess my sixteenth birthday was the day my brother and I became best friends and I learned a life's lesson: Never assume the worst of a person; always presume the best.

1. respite: (n) a usually short interval of rest or relief; (v) to delay; to postpone
2. contrite: (adj) feeling regret or sorrow for one's sins or offenses; penitent
3. stipulate: (v) to promise, in making an agreement; to require as an essential condition in making an agreement

Answers

1. contrite
2. respite
3. stipulate

Post-test—CVCe

Indicate how many syllables are in each word. If the word can be divided into syllables, indicate how it is divided.

Example: trispen   2   tris * pen

1. stipulate   _____
2. sublime   _____
3. apconstrate   _____
4. confiscate   _____
5. strappline   _____
6. bacquire   _____
7. incontrive   _____
8. splabe   _____
9. abgruve   _____
10. yatprane   _____

Write the words that your teacher dictates for each question.

1. _____   6. _____
2. _____   7. _____
3. _____   8. _____
4. _____   9. _____
5. _____   10. _____

Read the following passage orally.

The <u>Bewite</u> and the <u>Crane</u>

A <u>bewite</u> who had a <u>bone</u> stuck in his <u>thrope</u> hired a <u>crane</u>, for a large sum, to put her head into his <u>stamope</u> and <u>brine</u> out the bone. When the <u>crane</u> had <u>extracted</u> the <u>bone</u> and <u>demanded</u> the <u>prise</u> <u>tament</u>, the <u>bewife</u>, <u>grinning</u> and <u>gending</u> his teeth, exclaimed: "Why, you have <u>alrede</u> had a <u>gralate</u> <u>recomproze</u>, in been <u>permitted</u> to <u>strake</u> out your <u>shede</u> in safety from the <u>stamope</u> and jaws of a <u>bewife</u>." In <u>serping</u> the <u>wicked</u>, <u>expect</u> no <u>reward</u>, and be <u>thankful</u> if you <u>escape</u> <u>injury</u> for your <u>stanes</u>.

Answers

1. stipulate   <u>3</u>   stip * u * late
2. sublime   <u>2</u>   sub * lime
3. apconstrate   <u>3</u>   ap * con * strate
4. confiscate   <u>3</u>   con * fis * cate
5. strappline   <u>2</u>   strap * pline
6. bacquire   <u>2</u>   bac * quire
7. incontrive   <u>3</u>   in * con * trive
8. splabe   <u>1</u>   splabe
9. abgruve   <u>2</u>   ab * gruve
10. yatprane   <u>2</u>   yet * prane

1. fran * dale   6. slent * bule_
2. contrist   7. as * ken * ope
3. bri * gile   8. grat * tone
4. cloz * zip * ale   9. sis * tun * ode
5. yub * bin * ape   10. flog * ga * fine

The <u>Be * wite</u> and the <u>Crane</u>

A <u>be * wite</u> who had a <u>bone</u> stuck in his <u>thrope</u> hired a <u>crane</u>, for a large sum, to put her head into his <u>sta * mope</u> and <u>brine</u> out the bone. When the <u>crane</u> had <u>ex * trac * ted</u> the <u>bone</u> and <u>de * man * ded</u> the <u>prise</u> <u>ta * ment</u>, the <u>be * wife</u>, <u>grin * ning</u> and <u>gen * ding</u> his teeth, exclaimed: "Why, you have <u>al * rede</u> had a <u>gra * late</u> <u>re * com * proze</u>, in been <u>per * mit * ted</u> to <u>strake</u> out your <u>shede</u> in safety from the <u>sta * mope</u> and jaws of a <u>be * wife</u>." In <u>ser * ping</u> the <u>wic * ked</u>, <u>ex * pect</u> no <u>re * ward</u>, and be <u>thank * ful</u> if you <u>es * cape</u> <u>in * jur * y</u> for your <u>stanes</u>.

Scoring: Number of underlined words correct   /33

Chap·ter 8
Adding Suffixes

Sequence	Suggested Time Frame	Moving to Automaticity	Time	Materials
Week 8: Adding Suffixes	Day 1	Do-now	10 min.	Suffix fill-in-the-blanks #1
	Day 1	Mini-lesson	15 min.	Suffix cards #1, two-way suffix graphic organizer
	Day 2	Do-now	10 min.	Suffix fill-in-the-blanks #2
	Day 2	Mini-lesson from Day 1 cont'd.	15 min.	Suffix cards #1, two-way suffix graphic organizer
	Day 3	Do-now	10 min.	Root/suffix match #1
	Day 3	Guided Practice	15 min.	Category cards, suffix cards #2, four blank index cards per pair of students
	Day 3 or 4	Game—Ing	15 min.	"Ing" cards
	Day 4	Do-now	10 min.	Root/suffix match #2
	Day 4	Independent Practice	15 min.	Suffix worksheet
	Day 5	Do-now	10 min.	Root/suffix chart
	Day 5	Post-test	20 min.	Post-test—Suffixes

Week 8

Do-now 🖸 Chapter 8:
Suffix fill-in-the-blanks #1

Suffix fill-in-the-blanks #1

Add the suffix "y," "er," "est," or "ing" to each root word in parentheses to make the sentence make sense. Make any necessary changes to the root word to spell the new word correctly.

1. The air was _____ (smoke) because of the forest fire.
2. My mother was _____ (shake) her head no before I even finished the question.
3. I loved the movie because it was really _____ (scare).
4. The sun is _____ (shine) and it is a beautiful day to spend outside.
5. That picture is _____ (cute) than the other one.
6. Einstein was probably one of the _____ (smart) men who ever lived.

Answers

1. smoky
2. shaking
3. scary
4. shining
5. cuter
6. smartest

Mini-lesson 🖸 Chapter 8: Suffix cards #1
Chapter 8: Two-way suffix graphic organizer

Note: You can do this exercise on both Days 1 and 2.
- **Time:** 15 minutes on two days.
- **Goal:** To add a variety of suffixes to root words.
- **Materials:** Suffix cards #1, two-way suffix graphic organizer.
- **Overview:** Understand how suffixes help determine the meanings of words.

Directions

Have students think-pair-share a list of suffixes. Some possible suffixes are listed below. The list below is not complete, but it includes many of the common suffixes.

Suffix cards #1

ing	ed	ful	ness	able	ly
s, es	er	est	or	tion	al
y	ty	ic	ous	en	ive
less	ment	ize	ite	ist	ism
ish	hood	ant	age	ence	ess

Place the two-way suffix graphic organizer on the overhead or board. Using the suffix cards on the previous page, begin by placing "ing" and "ed" on the left side, and "ful" on the right side. Have students attempt to place suffixes on the appropriate side without explaining the rule. Students should notice that suffixes beginning in a vowel are on the left and those beginning with a consonant are on the right. When a student thinks he has determined the pattern, have him place the next syllable in the appropriate section.

Suffixes beginning with vowels: ing, ed, able, ess, ence, age, ant, ish, ize, ite, ist, ism, y, ic, ous, en, ive, es, er, est, or, al

Suffixes beginning with consonants: ful, ness, ly, tion, ty, less, ment, hood

Two-way suffix graphic organizer

Suffixes beginning with vowels	Suffixes beginning with consonants

Students are often confused about how to add a suffix to a root word, especially when working with a one-syllable word. The first rule they need to learn is the 1-1 rule. If there is one vowel in the word followed by one consonant, double the final consonant before adding a suffix that begins with a vowel. If the suffix begins with a consonant, do not double the final consonant of the root word. Model this rule by adding "ing" and "ed" to the first four words below. Have students work in pairs to complete the last four words.

sip	sipping, sipped	dent	denting, dented
pat	patting, patted	camp	camping, camped
rip	ripping, ripped	boast	boasting, boasted
trim	trimming, trimmed	spill	spilling, spilled

Remind students that, in English, "x" is an unusual letter and is never doubled at the end of a word.

Also remind them that when the root word ends in an "e," the "e" is dropped before suffixes that begin with a vowel but is not dropped before suffixes beginning with consonants. In words that end in the letter "y," the "y" changes to "i" and then the suffix is added, unless the suffix begins with "i." Model the rule with two of the following words and then have the students work in pairs to add suffixes to the rest of the words.

bake   baking, baker
flake   flaking, flaked
hope   hoping, hoped   hope   hopeful
state   stating, stated   state   statement, stately
pride   priding, prided   pride   prideful
try   trying, tried

Understanding suffixes can also help students determine the meaning of unknown words. The most common suffixes are "s," "es," "ed," and "ing." Your students will be familiar with "s" and "es," which are used to form the plurals of most nouns. The suffixes "ed" and "ing" are added to verbs to change their tense. Most students would have learned these suffixes in the primary grades. So at the secondary level, we really only need to focus on the spelling rather than the meaning of these suffixes.

Knowing the part of speech of the less typical suffixes will help your students determine meanings of unknown words. The noun suffixes include: "age," "al," "ance," "ant," "ate," "ee," "ence," "ent," "er," "or," "ar," "ese," "ess," "hood," "ice," "ism," "ist," "ment," "ness," "sion," "tain," "tion," and "ure." When students see a word with these endings, they know the new word is a person, place, or thing.

The following suffixes indicate adjectives: "able," "al," "er," "est," "ette," "let," "ful," "fully," "ible," "ic," "ical," "ish," "ive," "less," "ous," "some," and "worthy." These would be words that describe a noun.

The adverb suffixes are: "ly," "wards," "ways," "wide," and "wise." These would be words that describe verbs, adjectives, and other adverbs. The suffixes that create a verb are: "ate," "ed," "en," "ing," "ise," and "ize."

Day 2

Do-now   Chapter 8:
Suffix fill-in-the-blanks #2

Suffix fill-in-the-blanks #2
Add a suffix to the word in parentheses to make the sentence make sense. Make any changes you need to spell the new word correctly.

1. Our football team is _____ (try) to win the county championship.
2. Those red roses are the _____ (pretty) ones in our garden.
3. I am _____ apply) for a job at McDonalds so that I can have some spending money.
4. That _____ (mystery) man was the main character in the book.
5. He was _____ (employ) at the store last year.
6. I am _____ (envy) of my friend's long, straight, blonde hair.

Answers

1. trying
2. prettiest
3. applying
4. mysterious
5. employed
6. envious

Day 3

Do-now
Chapter 8: Root/suffix match #1

Root/suffix match #1

Draw a line from one word in the left column to one suffix in the right column to make a word that makes sense. Use each part one time. Make any necessary changes to the root word and write the new word correctly in the third column.

Root	Suffix	New Word
joy	ing	
smoke	ment	
grime	est	
big	ous	
hope	y	
govern	ful	

Answers

Root	Suffix	New Word
joy	ing	joyous
smoke	ment	smoking
grime	est	grimy
big	ous	biggest
hope	y	hopeful
govern	ful	government

Guided Practice

Chapter 8: Category cards
Chapter 8: Suffix cards #2

- **Time:** Fifteen minutes on one day.
- **Goal:** To understand how suffixes impact the root word's meaning.
- **Materials:** Category cards, suffix cards #2, four blank index cards per pair of students.
- **Overview:** Categorize suffixes by meaning.

Category cards

Person, Place, or Thing	Describes a Person, Place, or Thing	Describes the Verb, Adjective, or Another Adverb	The Action

Directions

Give each student a copy of the chart on the following page. Have the students cut the cards apart. Students should divide the suffixes into the four categories. The markings on the cards make it easy to check students' work. The suffixes for the person, place, or thing category (nouns) have a circle in the corner. The suffixes that describe a person, place, or thing (adjectives) have a square in the corner. The suffixes that describe the verb, adjective, or another adverb (adverbs) have an oval in the corner. The action suffixes (verbs) have a "v" in the corner.

After sorting the cards, have the pairs choose one suffix from each of the four categories and write the newly formed words on their index cards. Have students post their index cards on a bulletin board divided into the four categories.

Suffix cards #2

○ age	○ al	○ ance	○ ant	○ ate
○ ence	○ ent	○ er	○ or	○ ar
○ ess	○ hood	○ ism	○ ment	○ ness
□ able	□ est	□ ful	□ ic	□ ish
□ less	□ ous	□ some	□ worthy	□ ive
⬭ ly	⬭ wards	⬭ ways	⬭ wide	⬭ wise
v ate	v ed	v en	v ing	v ize

Game—Ing

Note: This game can take place on either Day 3 or 4.

- **Time:** Fifteen minutes on one day.
- **Goal:** To correctly add the "ing" suffix to a root word.
- **Materials:** "Ing" cards.
- **Overview:** Two to five students turn over cards to make a word that has an ing suffix on it.
- **Objective:** To win the game by forming words worth more points than your opponent's –ing words.

Directions

1. All cards are placed face down in a pile in the center of the table.
2. The first player chooses the top five cards and turns them over.
3. The player combines those cards in such a way as to correctly spell a word or words with the suffix "ing." These combinations are placed on the table in front of him.
4. Words that are formed using two cards are worth two points, and those that are formed using three cards are worth three points.
5. The player's turn ends when all the possible combinations have been formed.
6. He then places any unused cards face up and to the right of his played cards.
7. The next player chooses five cards from either the pile of face down cards in the center of the table or from those unused face up in front of any of his opponents.
8. Play continues counterclockwise around the table with the next player combining cards in such a way as to correctly spell words with the "ing" suffix.
9. The game ends when there are less then five cards left unused anywhere on the table.

Day 4

Do-now

Root/suffix match #2

Draw a line from one word in the left column to one suffix in the right column to make a word that makes sense. Use each part one time. Make any necessary changes to the root word and write the new word correctly in the third column.

Root	Suffix	New Word
state	ing	
dispute	less	
bone	able	
like	ty	
compete	hood	
safe	wise	

Answers

Root	Suffix	New Word
state	ing	statehood
dispute	less	disputable
bone	able	boneless
like	ty	likewise
compete	hood	competing
safe	wise	safety

Independent Practice

Chapter 8:
Suffix worksheet

- **Time:** Fifteen minutes on one day.
- **Goal:** To correctly spell words containing the "ing" suffix.
- **Materials:** Suffix worksheet.
- **Overview:** Individually, students complete the worksheet.

Suffix worksheet

Directions

Underline the vowel. Circle the consonant after the vowel. If the word has only one vowel and one consonant, double the final consonant before adding the "ing" suffix. Write the entire word. Never double an "x."

camp	_____	fit	_____
plaster	_____	slip	_____
trim	_____	last	_____
slam	_____	bend	_____
float	_____	shop	_____
bask	_____	dream	_____
drop	_____	roam	_____
rent	_____	box	_____

If the root word ends in an "e," drop the "e" before a suffix beginning with a vowel. If the suffix begins with a consonant, the silent "e" remains. If the root word ends with a "y," add "ing." Remember, with other suffixes, the "y" may change to "i" before the suffix. Write each root word two times, once with each of the indicated suffixes.

Root Word	Vowel Suffix	Consonant Suffix
propose	(ing) _____	(s) _____
sled	(ing) _____	(s) _____
hope	(ing) _____	(ful) _____
try	(ing) _____	(s) _____
compose	(ing) _____	(s) _____
care	(ing) _____	(ful) _____
drip	(ing) _____	(less) _____
marry	(ing) _____	(s) _____
combine	(ing) _____	(s) _____

Use five of the above words with suffixes in sentences.

_____

_____

_____

_____

_____

_____

Answers

camp	camping	fit	fitting
plaster	plastering	slip	slipping
trim	trimming	last	lasting
slam	slamming	bend	bending
float	floating	shop	shopping
bask	basking	dream	dreaming
drop	dropping	roam	roaming
rent	renting	box	boxing
propose	(ing) proposing	(s)	proposes
sled	(ing) sledding	(s)	sleds
hope	(ing) hoping	(ful)	hopeful
try	(ing) trying	(s)	tries
compose	(ing) composing	(s)	composes
care	(ing) caring	(ful)	careful
drip	(ing) dripping	(less)	dripless
marry	(ing) marrying	(s)	marries
combine	(ing) combining	(s)	combines

Answers will vary.

_____

_____

_____

_____

_____

_____

_____

Day 5

Do-now Chapter 8:
Root/suffix chart

Root/suffix chart

Complete the chart below.

Root Word	er	ness	ly	ed	est	ity
bare				=======		=======
pale						=======
scarce				=======		
brave						
sincere				=======		=======

Answers

Root Word	er	ness	ly	ed	est	ity
bare	barer	bareness	barely	=======	barest	=======
pale	paler	paleness	palely	paled	palest	=======
scarce	scarcer	scarceness	scarcely	=======	scarcest	scarcity
brave	braver	braveness	bravely	braved	bravest	=====
sincere	sincerer	sincereness	sincerely	=======	sincerest	sincerity

Post-test—Suffixes

Add the indicated suffix to the root word and indicate the category of the new word.
Example: joy (ous) joyous: describes a person, place, or thing

1. compose (ing) _____
2. slam (ed) _____
3. state (hood) _____
4. contest (able) _____
5. care (ful) _____
6. history (ic) _____
7. scare (y) _____
8. try (s) _____
9. energy (ize) _____
10. hop (ing) _____

1. _____   6. _____
2. _____   7. _____
3. _____   8. _____
4. _____   9. _____
5. _____   10. _____

Write the word your teacher dictates.

Read the following passage orally.

The Propiper Piping

A propiper took his flute and grabed it by his droxes at the seashore. Spranding on a
rock projecting into the sea, he played several draces hoping that the fish, attracted by his
composition, would jump into the droxes which he had pladed below. At last after thrating
and thrating, he drepped his flute aside, and began trossing his drox into the water. Fleing a
propiper, he had an excessive amount of fish. When he saw them caping about in the drox
he said: "O you pressive creatures, when I piped you would not dance, but now that I have
broped you do so merrily."

Answers

1. compose (ing)   <u>composing</u>   <u>action</u>
2. slam (ed)   <u>slammed</u>   <u>the action</u>
3. state (hood)   <u>statehood</u>   <u>person, place, or thing</u>
4. contest (able)   <u>contestable</u>   <u>describes a person, place, or thing</u>
5. care (ful)   <u>careful</u>   <u>describes a person, place, or thing</u>
6. history (ic)   <u>historic</u>   <u>describes a person, place, or thing</u>
7. scare (y)   <u>scary</u>   <u>describes a person, place, or thing</u>
8. try (s)   <u>tries</u>   <u>the action</u>
9. energy (ize)   <u>energize</u>   <u>the action</u>
10. hop (ing)   <u>hopping</u>   <u>the action</u>

1. <u>cherries</u>		6. <u>camped</u>
2. <u>mysterious</u>		7. <u>boating</u>
3. <u>ridding</u>		8. <u>gladden</u>
4. <u>marrying</u>		9. <u>flipped</u>
5. <u>trading</u>		10. <u>finalize</u>

The <u>Pro * pi * per</u> <u>Pi * ping</u>

A <u>pro * pi * per</u> took his flute and <u>gra * bed</u> it by his <u>drox * es</u> at the seashore. <u>Spran * ding</u> on a rock <u>pro * jec * ting</u> into the sea, he played several <u>dra * ces</u> <u>ho * ping</u> that the fish, <u>at * trac * ted</u> by his <u>com * po * si * tion</u>, would jump into the <u>drox * es</u> which he had <u>pla * ded</u> below. At last after <u>thra * ting</u> and <u>thra * ting</u>, he <u>drep * ped</u> his flute aside, and began <u>tros * sing</u> his drox into the water. <u>Fle * ing</u> a <u>pro * pi * per,</u> he had an <u>ex * ces * sive</u> amount of fish. When he saw them <u>ca * ping</u> about in the drox he said: "O you <u>pres * sive</u> creatures, when I <u>pi * ped</u> you would not dance, but now that I have <u>bro * ped</u> you do so <u>mer * ri * ly</u>."

Scoring: Number of underlined words correct   /25

Chap·ter 9
CVVC Syllable

Sequence	Suggested Time Frame	Moving to Automaticity	Time	Materials
Week 9: CVVC— digraphs	Day 1	Do-now	10 min.	Vowel combination prompts
	Day 1	Mini-lesson	15 min.	Vowel team words
	Day 2	Do-now	10 min.	Homonym practice
	Day 2	Guided Practice	15 min.	Whiteboards, single- and multiple-syllable vowel digraph cards
	Day 3	Do-now	10 min.	Vowel combination word scramble
	Day 3	Guided Practice from Day 2 cont'd.	15 min.	Whiteboards, single- and multiple-syllable vowel digraph cards
	Day 4	Do-now	10 min.	CVVC rhyme
	Day 4	Game—Winning Teams	20 min.	Vowel team cards, classroom white board
	Day 5	Do-now	10 min.	
	Day 5	Extension	20 min.	Vowel team cards, class white board
	Day 5	Independent Practice	20 min.	Vowel team worksheet
Week 10: CVVC— oi/oy, ou/ow	Day 1	Do-now	10 min.	Diphthong fill-in-the-blanks #1
	Day 1	Mini-lesson	15 min.	Paper and pencil
	Day 2	Do-now	10 min.	Syllable matching #1
	Day 2	Guided Practice	15 min.	Diphthong cards, word sort graphic organizer, word sort list, white boards, dry erase markers
	Day 3	Do-now	10 min.	Diphthong fill-in-the-blanks #2
	Day 3	Guided Practice from Day 2 cont'd.	15 min.	Diphthong cards, word sort graphic organizer, word sort list, white boards, dry erase markers
	Day 4	Do-now	10 min.	Syllable matching #2
	Day 4	Game—Racing Fever	20 min.	Die, place holders for the game, Racing Fever word cards, Racing Fever game board
	Day 4 or 5	Extension	20 min.	Die, place holders for the game, Racing Fever game board, Racing Fever word cards
	Day 5	Do-now	10 min.	Diphthong fill-in-the-blanks #3
	Day 5	Independent Practice	20 min.	Diphthong worksheet

Week 11: CVVC— au/aw	Day 1	Do-now	10 min.	Diphthong fill-in-the-blanks #4
	Day 1	Mini-lesson	20 min.	Classroom white board, example "au/aw" words
	Day 2	Do-now	10 min.	Syllable prompts
	Day 2	Guided Practice	20 min.	Set of "au/aw" cards for each student
	Day 3	Do-now	10 min.	Syllable matching #3
	Day 3	Game—"AU/AW" Password	20 min.	One checkbook cover for each player; Password set A, set B, and help cards for each team
	Day 4	Do-now	10 min.	Syllable matching #4
	Day 4	Independent Practice	20 min.	"aw/au" word search
	Day 5	Do-now	10 min.	Syllable count
	Day 5	Post-test	20 min.	Post-test—CVVC

Week 9

Day 1

Do-now

Chapter 9:
Vowel combination prompts

Underline the double vowel combination in the first word in each row. Use the vowel combination from the first word in each row to form a new second word. Choose any two words and use them in a sentence.

Prompt

billow	pill_ _
frail	tr_ _ l
destroy	empl _ _
please	dis _ _ se
speed	overs _ _
throat	cr _ _ k

Mini-lesson

Chapter 9:
Vowel team words

- **Time:** Fifteen minutes on one day.
- **Goal:** To establish awareness of words with vowel team combinations.
- **Materials:** Vowel team words.
- **Overview:** Read, write, and underline the vowel team in given words.

Directions

The last type of syllable is the CVVC syllable. Students will probably remember learning in elementary school the poem, "When two vowels go walking, the first one does the talking." This rule applies to those times when two vowels together form a single long sound. Remind students that "y" and "w" can sometimes act as either vowels or consonants.

The CVVC vowel team combinations that form the long vowel sound include "ai," "ay," "ee," "ea," "ew," "ey," "ie," "oa," "oe," and "ue." The "ow" combination should also be included, when it makes the long vowel sound, as in the word "snow." Students usually do not have too much difficulty with these combinations.

Display the following single and multisyllabic words with vowel teams. Read the single-syllable words in List 1 and have students write the words and circle the vowel combinations. Read the multisyllabic words in List 2 and have students write the words, divide them into syllables, and circle the vowel teams.

Vowel team words

List 1		List 2	
train	tr(ai)n	explain	ex * pl(ai)n
play		decay	
beet		freedom	
treat		appeal	
grew		jewel	
key		alley	
true		barbeque	
hoe		aloe	
pie		diehard	
throat		approach	
snow		arrow	

Answers

List 1		List 2	
train	tr(ai)n	explain	ex * pl(ai)n
pl(ay)		decay	de * c(ay)
b(ee)t		freedom	fr(ee) * dom
tr(ea)t		appeal	ap * p(ea)l
gr(ew)		jewel	j(ew) * el
k(ey)		alley	al * l(ey)
tr(ue)		barbeque	bar * be * q(ue)
h(oe)		aloe	al * (oe)
p(ie)		diehard	d(ie) * hard
thr(oa)t		approach	ap * pr(oa)ch
sn(ow)		arrow	ar * r(ow)

Do-now

Homonym practice

The words below are homonyms. Circle the double vowel combinations in the words below, and then use the homonyms in the sentences.

flee, flea   sail, sale

crews, cruise   wail, whale

1. The _____ ship tried to _____ from the incoming hurricane.
2. At the garage _____ I bought a large, blue, blow-up fish that looked like a _____ for our swimming pool.
3. The _____ readied their _____ing boats for the upcoming race.
4. Our dog _____ed like a baby when we gave him a _____ bath to rid him of the nasty little bugs.

Answers

fl(ee), fl(ea)   (sail) sale

cr(ew)s, cr(ui)se   w(ai)l, whale

1. The <u>cruise</u> ship tried to <u>flee</u> from the incoming hurricane.
2. At the garage <u>sale</u> I bought a large, blue, blow-up fish that looked like a <u>whale</u> for our swimming pool.
3. The <u>crews</u> readied their <u>sail</u>ing boats for the upcoming race.
4. Our dog <u>wail</u>ed like a baby when we gave him a <u>flea</u> bath to rid him of the nasty little bugs.

Guided Practice

Note: You can do this exercise on both Days 2 and 3.
- **Time:** Fifteen minutes on two days.
- **Goal:** To encode and decode single and multisyllabic words with vowel digraphs.
- **Materials:** Whiteboards, single- and multiple-syllable vowel digraph cards.
- **Overview:** Read words containing vowel digraphs and write them from dictation.

Directions

Cut apart the words on the chart on the following page. Students work in pairs to practice reading the cards. Collect the cards and dictate the single and multisyllabic words with vowel digraphs to students. The student teams should write the words on their individual white boards. Each pair of students earns a point for each word they spell correctly.

Single-syllable vowel digraph cards

cream	street	pail	toast	coach	beam
hair	faint	team	braid	suit	cue
hail	creek	coast	throat	poach	aloe
bait	dew	yeast	bleak	drew	fruit
juice	cruise	slew	tray	spray	hue
hay	snail	preen	train	tweed	seal

Multiple-syllable vowel digraph cards

complaint	payment	daisy	retainer	proclaim	defray
prevail	bailiff	impairment	obtain	dainty	assail
abstain	ailment	restrain	parakeet	tweezers	domineer
proceed	breech	canteen	racketeer	discreet	indeed
freedom	volunteer	jamboree	revenue	parsley	engineer
construe	esteem	trolley	hockey	baloney	medley

As with most rules, there are exceptions. Explain to students that the first step in decoding an unknown word with what appears to be a vowel team is to try saying the vowel combination with a long vowel sound. Share the following words: "cruel," "influence," "koala," and "fuel." The vowel combinations in these words don't work as a team. The vowels work independently and are actually in separate syllables.

In pairs, have students divide the following words into syllables: "violent," "diet," "influence," "leotard," "liar," "museum," and "nucleus." Note that the vowels are used in separate syllables.

Remind students that the vowel combination "ie" is often found at the end of words where the "y" has been changed to "i" to form the plural of a word or the comparative form of a word, for example, "exemplifies," "sillier," and "silliest." Students will also notice that in many words the "ie" team forms a completely different sound, as in "friend," "fiend," or "fierce." In addition, the "ey" team is often found at the end of words to form the long /e/ sound, as in "hockey," "mopey," and "tomatoey."

Day 3

Do-now
Chapter 9:
Vowel combination word scramble

Vowel combination word scramble
Unscramble the following letters to form words with vowel combinations. Use one of the words in a sentence.

Scrambled Words	Answers
adiys	daisy
opplee	people
eregn	green
nradi	drain
iirans	raisin

Guided Practice
Continue from Day 2.

Day 4

Do-now   Chapter 9: CVVC rhyme

CVVC rhyme

Read the classic rhyme below and underline the CVVC words. Remember consonant blends and digraphs count as one sound. "Fl," for example, would be represented by the letter "c."

Rain, rain, go away,
Come again another day.
Little Johnny wants to play;
Rain, rain, go to Spain,
Never show your face again!

Answers

<u>Rain</u>, <u>rain</u> go <u>away</u>,
Come <u>again</u> another <u>day</u>.
Little Johnny wants to <u>play</u>;
<u>Rain</u>, <u>rain</u>, go to <u>Spain</u>,
Never <u>show</u> your face <u>again</u>!

Game—Winning Teams   Chapter 9: Vowel team cards

- **Time:** Twenty minutes on one day.
- **Goal:** To correctly write words containing vowel digraphs.
- **Materials:** Vowel team cards, classroom white board.
- **Overview:** Teams of three to five students write words containing specified vowel digraphs.
- **Objective:** To be the team to get the most points in the relay.

Directions

1. The class is divided into teams of four players.
2. Each team has a set of vowel team cards. The cards are shuffled and placed face down in a pile in front of each team.
3. The first person on each team turns over the top card.
4. That person reads the vowel team on the card and runs up to the board and writes a word containing that vowel team.
5. If the player is having difficulty coming up with a word, teammates may help the player.
6. After the first team member writes the word on the board, the player goes back and tags the hand of the next team member.
7. The second team member turns over the next card, goes to the board, and writes a word containing the next vowel team.
8. The first team to finish with the most correctly spelled words is the winning team.

Do-now

Using a poetry book from your classroom library, rewrite a poem you like and highlight each of the double vowel combination words.

Extension 🔘 Chapter 9:
Vowel team cards

- **Time:** Twenty minutes on one day.
- **Goal:** To correctly write words containing vowel digraphs, prefixes, and suffixes.
- **Materials:** Vowel team cards, classroom white board.
- **Overview:** Teams of three to five students write words containing specified vowel digraphs, prefixes, and suffixes.

Directions

After the students are successful writing the individual words on the board, they could play a second round and add a prefix or a suffix to the word they wrote on the board in round one.

Independent Practice 🔘 Chapter 9:
Vowel team worksheet

- **Time:** Twenty minutes on one day.
- **Goal:** To supply missing vowel teams in specified words and to use these words in context.
- **Materials:** Vowel team worksheet.
- **Overview:** Individually, students supply missing vowel teams and then create a story containing the words.

Vowel team worksheet
Directions

Write the missing vowel team in each word.

incr _ _ se	aven _ _	b _ _ st	r _ _
gl _ _ t	compl _ _ n	betr _ _	accl _ _ m
constr _ _ nt	refer _ _	donk _ _	tw _ _ zers
commit _ _	racket _ _ r	balon _ _	f _ _ lure
abst _ _ n	proc _ _ d	ren_ _al	appr _ _ sal
dom _ _ n	fr _ _ dom	parak _ _ t	parsl _ _
est _ _ m	engin _ _ r	ind _ _ d	medl _ _
dism _ _	ret _ _ n	volunt _ _ r	_ _ lment

Write a story using ten of the above words.

_____

_____

_____

_____

_____

Answers

incr <u>e a</u> se	aven <u>u e</u>	b <u>e a</u> st/b <u>o a</u> st	r <u>a y</u>
gl <u>o a</u> t	compl <u>a i</u> n	betr <u>a y</u>	accl <u>a i</u> m
constr <u>a i</u> nt	refer <u>e e</u>	donk <u>e y</u>	tw <u>e e</u> zers
commit <u>e e</u>	racket <u>e e</u> r	balon <u>e y</u>	f <u>a i</u> lure
abst <u>a i</u> n	proc <u>e e</u> d	ren <u>e w</u> al	appr <u>a i</u> sal
dom <u>a i</u> n	fr <u>e e</u> dom	parak <u>e e</u> t	parsl <u>e y</u>
est <u>e e</u> m	engin <u>e e</u> r	ind <u>e e</u> d	medl <u>e y</u>
dism <u>a y</u>	ret <u>a i</u> n	volunt <u>e e</u> r	<u>a i</u> lment

Write a story using ten of the above words.

Answers will vary.

Week 10

Day 1

Do-now Chapter 9:
Diphthong fill-in-the-blanks #1

Diphthong fill-in-the-blanks #1

Complete the following words with the diphthong "oi" or "oy."

empl _ _   app_ _nt

destr _ _   sp_ _l

enj_ _   tops_ _l

j_ _ ful   n_ _ seless

dec_ _   inv_ _ce

Look at the words you just created. In a syllable, where do you generally find the "oy" vowel combination? Where do you usually find the "oi" vowel combination?

Mini-lesson

- **Time:** Fifteen minutes on one day.
- **Goal:** To understand how the placement in a syllable impacts the spelling of the vowel diphthongs "oi" and "oy."
- **Materials:** Paper and pencil.
- **Overview:** Read, sort, and generate words with "oi" and "oy" combinations.

Directions

Sometimes when two vowels are together they do not make a short or a long vowel sound; instead, they make a totally different sound. Two of the easiest vowel diphthong combinations are "oi" and "oy." Students seem to understand the sound that these combinations make, but they have some difficulty determining when to use which vowel combination in their writing.

When teaching this diphthong, help students identify when each combination is used. The "oi" combination tends to be used in the middle of the syllable, and the "oy" combination tends to be used at the end of the syllable.

Say the following words aloud, and after each word, ask students to indicate if they hear the /oi/ sound in the middle or at the end of the syllable. Then write the words on the board and allow students to see the vowel combinations and their placement.

appoint, embroider, boy, annoy, coin, corduroy, oyster

Divide the class into four groups. Number the groups 1, 2, 3, and 4. Allow five minutes for each group to come up with six of the most unusual words they can think of containing the /oi/ sound. Students may use whatever resources are in the room. When time is called, have group 1 dictate the first word on their list to group 2, who indicates whether the /oi/ sound would be spelled "oi" or "oy." If the group answers correctly, they earn one point for their team. Group 2 dictates one of their words to group 3. Play continues in this fashion until all words are dictated. If a word on the team's list has already been dictated, they must cross it off their list and they lose one turn. Words cannot be repeated.

Day 2

Do-now

Syllable matching #1

Match the syllable on the left with the syllable on the right. Choose one word and use it in a sentence.

moist	ploy
a	point
ap	en
de	al
des	troy
en	joy
roy	void

Answers

moisten

avoid

appoint

deploy

destroy

enjoy

royal

Guided Practice

Chapter 9: Diphthong cards
Chapter 9: Word sort graphic organizer
Chapter 9: Word sort list

Note: You can do this exercise on Days 2 and 3.
- **Time:** Fifteen minutes on two days.
- **Goal:** To understand how the placement in a syllable impacts the spelling of the vowel diphthongs "oi," "oy," "ou," and "ow."
- **Materials:** Diphthong cards, word sort graphic organizer, word sort list, white boards, dry erase markers.
- **Overview:** Read and sort words with diphthong combinations.

Directions

Begin by having students divide their individual white boards into two columns, "oi" and "oy." Dictate the words from the diphthong cards on the following page and have students write each word in the appropriate column. Remind students that the /oi/ sound in the middle of the syllable is generally formed with the letters "oi," and that at the end of the syllable it is generally formed with the letters "oy." If the word is multisyllabic, instruct students to divide the word into syllables. Sometimes the CVVC syllable may not have an initial or final consonant.

Diphthong cards

soil	annoy	appoint	broiler	poison
joint	choice	ointment	oyster	destroy
rejoice	joint	avoid	joy	spoil
moist	joyous	voice	convoy	noisy
paranoid	croin	deploy	thyroid	turmoil
foyer	devoid	boycott	flamboyant	exploitation
alloy	loitering	loyalty	employment	overjoy
toilet	enjoy	royal	loyal	join

Once students understand the "oi/oy" rule, they will find the rules for other diphthongs easier because the rules are similar. The next activity focuses on the diphthongs "ou" and "ow" when they make the same sound. The combination "ow" is often used at the end of the syllable and before the letters "n," "k," and "l," while "ou" tends to be used in the middle of the syllable. This rule will help students determine which vowel combination to use in their writing.

Dictate the words below and ask students to listen for the /ou/ sound in the word. Then write the words on the board along with the rule: " 'ow' is often used at the end of the syllable and before the letters 'n,' 'k,' and 'l,' while 'ou' tends to be used in the middle of a syllable." Ask students to examine the words and how the rule applies to the words.

a * bound, ac * count, al * low, flow * er, pow * er, prowl,
a * bout, south, clown, foul, owl

Remind students that "ow" also makes the long /o/ sound as discussed in the lesson on vowel digraphs. In this lesson, the focus will be on the /ou/ sound of ow. Have students practice sorting the words into the appropriate section on the graphic organizer below. This can be completed on the overhead with the whole group or in pairs as a cooperative learning activity.

Word sort graphic organizer

OU	OW

Word sort list

owl	loud	bow	thousand	round	out
cow	clown	down	cloud	found	towel
couch	ground	vowel	surround	trousers	frown
around	shower	count	announce	drown	about
town	chowder	discount	powder	aloud	amount
drowsy	brow	allow	plow	sound	crouch
now	gown	shout	tower	lousy	allowance
rowdy	power	flower	crown	ouch	pounce
hound	scout	pound	mountain	fountain	mount
pout	mound	trowel	chowder	flounder	coward

Day 3

Do-now   Chapter 9:
Diphthong fill-in-the-blanks #2

Diphthong fill-in-the-blanks #2

Complete the following words with the vowel diphthongs "ou" or "ow."

c_ _ch	nightg_ _n	am_ _nt	backgr_ _nd	bl_ _se
sh_ _er	h_ _l	fr_ _n	sh_ _t	pr_ _ler

Choose any two of the words and use them in one sentence.

Guided Practice

Continue from Day 2.

Day 4

Do-now

Syllable matching #2

Match the syllable on the left with a syllable in the second column. Use the words in the sentences that follow.

drow	ledge	It was late at night and I had to pull off the road to sleep because I was beginning to feel _____.
coun	nounce	My teacher will often _____ me to help me make the right decisions.
know	sel	I registered for the online class with the _____ that I would have a lot of extra work to do at home.
moun	er	I love skiing, but the _____ I was about to ski down was so huge it scared me to death!
pro	tain	I slowly began to _____ the spelling word.
pow	sy	The boat lost _____ when it ran out of gas.

Answers

drowsy	It was late at night and I had to pull off the road to sleep because I was beginning to feel drowsy.
counsel	My teacher will often counsel me to help me make the right decisions.
knowledge	I registered for the online class with the knowledge that I would have a lot of extra work to do at home.
mountain	I love skiing but the mountain I was about to ski down was so huge it scared me to death!
pronounce	I slowly began to pronounce the spelling word.
power	The boat lost power when it ran out of gas.

Game—Racing Fever

Chapter 9: Racing Fever word cards
Chapter 9: Racing Fever game board

- **Time:** Twenty minutes on one day.
- **Goal:** To correctly spell words containing the "ou" and "ow" diphthongs.
- **Materials:** Die, place holders for the game, Racing Fever word cards, Racing Fever game board.
- **Overview:** Two to five players read and spell words as they move around a game board racetrack.
- **Objective:** To be the first player to reach the finish line.

Directions

1. Place the cards in a pile in the center of the table.
2. Each player rolls the die and the player who rolls the highest number goes first. The play continues to the right of that individual.
3. The person to the right of the first player turns over the top card and reads it to the first player.
4. The first player spells the word. If the player spells it correctly, he moves his marker to the next space on the board that contains the vowel diphthong in the word that he spelled ("ou" or "ow"). If the player does not spell it correctly, his turn ends.
5. The first player then rolls the die and moves that many more spaces.
6. If the player lands on a stop sign, the player loses a turn.
7. If the player lands on a car, the player gets an extra turn.
8. The play continues to the right of the first player.
9. Play continues in the same manner until someone reaches the finish line.

Extension

Chapter 9: Racing Fever game board
Chapter 9: Racing Fever word cards

Note: You can do this exercise on either Day 4 or 5.

- **Time:** Twenty minutes on one day.
- **Goal:** To correctly use words containing the "ou" and "ow" diphthongs in sentences.
- **Materials:** Die, place holders for the game, Racing Fever game board, Racing Fever word cards.
- **Overview:** Two to five players spell and use words in sentences as they move around a game board racetrack.

Directions

When students can easily spell the words, the game is made more difficult by having students spell the word and use it correctly in a sentence.

Day 5

Do-now 🔘 Chapter 9:
Diphthong fill-in-the-blanks #3

Diphthong fill-in-the-blanks #3

Name the "ow" or "ou" word.

1. This is a two-syllable word, containing "ow," for a thick soup made with clams or other fish and vegetables. The word is _ _ _ _ _ _ _.

2. This is a two-syllable word, containing "ow," describing a piece of cloth or paper used for drying. The word is _ _ _ _ _ .

3. This is a two-syllable word, containing "ou," that is used to describe a device used for catching an unwanted rodent. _ _ _ _ _ _ _ _ _

4. This is a one-syllable word beginning with "s," containing "ow," and meaning to frown in anger. _ _ _ _ _

5. This is a three syllable word beginning with "a," containing "ow," and meaning to recognize.

    _ _ _ _ _ _ _ _ _ _ _

Answers
1. chowder
2. towel
3. mousetrap
4. scowl
5. acknowledge

Independent Practice 🔘 Chapter 9:
Diphthong worksheet

- **Time:** Twenty minutes on one day.
- **Goal:** To decode words and use them appropriately in sentences.
- **Materials:** Diphthong worksheet.
- **Overview:** Individually, students read words and use them in sentences.

Diphthong worksheet

Directions

Use these words in the sentences that follow:

employed	route	avoid	accountant	corduroy	destroy
boisterous	voyage	cloudy	South	down	countertop
flowers	destroy	coin	mouth	snout	acknowledged
noise	allowance	crown	sour	growled	repositioned

1. I tried a different _____ to work, in an effort to _____ heavy traffic from road construction.

2. The _____ crowd made a lot of _____ leaving the championship game.

3. The _____ day wasn't going to _____ my fun at the beach!

4. I placed my last month's _____ on the _____ to see if I had sufficient funds for a new pair of _____ pants.

5. Riding my bike in the garden, I stuck to the pavement so I wouldn't _____ the _____ that lined the path.

6. The candy _____ looked good, but it left a _____ taste in my _____.

7. The king _____the queen by placing a diamond _____ on her head.

8. The angry dog _____ _____ and _____ while pulling back the lips of his _____.

9. The ship's crew prepared for a long _____ to _____ America.

10. The _____ was _____ by one of the top agencies in the city.

Answers

1. I tried a different _route_ to work, in an effort to _avoid_ heavy traffic from road construction.

2. The _boisterous_ crowd made a lot of _noise_ leaving the championship game.

3. The _cloudy_ day wasn't going to _destroy_ my fun at the beach!

4. I placed my last month's _allowance_ on the _countertop_ to see if I had sufficient funds for a new pair of _corduroy_ pants.

5. Riding my bike in the garden, I stuck to the pavement so I wouldn't _destroy_ the _flowers_ that lined the path.

6. The candy _coin_ looked good, but it left a _sour_ taste in my _mouth_.

7. The king _acknowledged_ the queen by placing a diamond _crown_ on her head.

8. The angry dog _crouched_ _down_ and _growled_ while pulling back the lips of his _snout_.

9. The ship's crew prepared for a long _voyage_ to _South_ America.

10. The _accountant_ was _employed_ by one of the top agencies in the city.

Week 11

Day 1

Do-now Chapter 9: Diphthong fill-in-the-blanks #4

Diphthong fill-in-the-blanks #4

Read the definition and fill in the missing letters to form the "au" or "aw" word being described.

1. s_ _ aw _: a loud cry that a bird might make

2. c_ _ _ _ aw: a cold salad made with shredded cabbage, mayonnaise, and sometimes shredded carrots

3. _au_ _ r: a small dish that sits beneath a coffee cup

4. s_ _aw_ y: really skinny

5. aw_ _ _ _ d: not graceful; clumsy

Answers

1. squawk
2. coleslaw
3. saucer
4. scrawny
5. awkward

Mini-lesson

- **Time:** Twenty minutes on one day.
- **Goal:** To correctly write words containing the "au/aw" diphthongs.
- **Materials:** Classroom white board, example "au/aw" words.
- **Overview:** Students will identify the rule for "au/aw."

Directions

The rule for "au" and "aw" is the same as the rule for "ou" and "ow." Once the students know the "ou/ow" rule, it can easily be applied the "au/aw" rule. The combination "au" is typically used at the beginning or in the middle of the syllable. The combination "aw" is typically used at the end of the syllable and before the letters "n," "k," and "l."

Display the rule on the board: "au" is generally used at the beginning or in the middle of the syllable; "aw" is generally used at the end of a syllable and before the letters "n," "k," and "l." Then write the following words on the board and ask students to explain how the rule applies to each word: autograph, argonaut, crawfish, awkward, fawn, shawl.

Do-now 🔘 Chapter 9:
Syllable prompts

Syllable prompts

Divide the following words into syllables. Use at least two of the words in a sentence.
Circle the "aw" or "au" syllable. Remember the "aw" and "au" teams each remain together as
one sound and that each syllable will have only one vowel sound. Then use at least one of the
words in a sentence. Use a dictionary if necessary.

auditorium	**Answers**	(au) * di * tor * i * um
tomahawk		tom * a * ha(wk)
authentic		(au) * then * tic
nautical		n(au) * ti * cal
autobiography		au * to *(bi)* og * ra * phy

Guided Practice 🔘 Chapter 9:
"au/aw" cards

- **Time:** Twenty minutes on one day.
- **Goal:** To correctly identify the vowel diphthong in specified words.
- **Materials:** Set of "au/aw" cards for each student.
- **Overview:** Students will hold up "au/aw" cards to indicate the correct spelling in dictated words.

Directions

Give each student an "au" and an "aw" card. Dictate a word from the list on the following page and have students hold up the card for the vowel combination that is in that word. Continue to dictate words until the students demonstrate the ability to identify the spelling used in the dictated words.

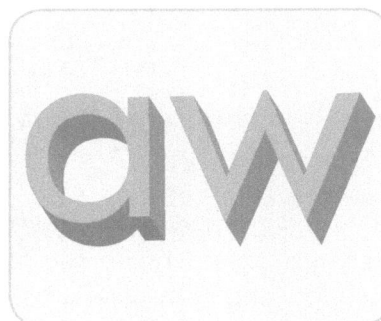

straw	law	saucer	sauce	squaw	draw
awkward	squawk	fault	drawn	launch	raw
autograph	faucet	laundry	astronaut	dawn	haunt
author	brawl	fawn	August	auto	scrawny
applaud	tomahawk	hawk	shawl	yawn	claw
exhaust	fraud	pawn	haul	flaunt	taut
jaunt	auditory	authentic	pauper	automate	fraudulent
augment	fauna	saucy	caucus	bauble	laundress
caustic	nautical	austere	hydraulic	auditor	hawthorn
dawdle	taunt	audience	coleslaw	sawmill	strawberry

Day 3

Do-now

Chapter 9:
Syllable matching #3

Syllable matching #3

Divide into syllables and read the "aw" or "au" word. Match the word with its definition. Check the dictionary to see if you are correct and then use one word in a sentence.

1. automate
2. fraudulent
3. augment
4. caustic
5. austere

a. serious looking; not fancy; strict
b. to make automatic
c. bitter; made of acid
d. to make larger; to increase
e. cheating; not honest; criminal

Answers

1. au * to * mate—b
2. frau * du * lant—e
3. aug * ment—d
4. caus * tic—c
5. aus * tere—a

Game—"AU/AW" Password

Chapter 9: Password set A cards
Chapter 9: Password set B cards
Chapter 9: Password help cards

- **Time:** Twenty minutes on one day.
- **Goal:** To identify an "au/aw" diphthong word from one-word clues.
- **Materials:** One checkbook cover for each player; Password set A, set B, and help cards for each team.
- **Overview:** Players will guess the word their team member is holding based on one-word clues.
- **Objective:** To guess the word your teammate is holding based on one-word clues.

Directions

1. Before play begins, make a copy of the Set A and Set B cards for each team and cut them apart.

2. Each team gets a checkbook cover. (These can usually be obtained from your local bank.)

3. Place one copy of Set A in two of the checkbooks and one copy of Set B in the other two checkbooks. One member of each team will have the Set A cards and the other member will have the Set B cards.

4. Play begins with the two players holding the Set A cards opening their card holder (checkbook cover) and looking at the first word. They will be taking turns giving clues to their teammates to see who can guess the word first.

5. Toss a coin to see who goes begins.

6. The first player gives a one-word clue to his teammate. If the teammate guesses the word after the initial clue, that team earns ten points.

7. If she does not guess the word correctly, play goes to the next team. The first player on team two gives a one-word clue to her teammate. This student thinks about the clue given by the opposing team and the clue given by his teammate and gets one chance to guess the word. If he guesses the word correctly, his team wins nine points.

8. If not, play goes back to the original player who gives another one-word clue. If his teammate guesses the word, their team earns eight points.

9. Play continues until someone guesses the correct word or there are no points left.

10. Everyone, or a game monitor, keeps track of the score.

11. Play then goes to the teammates who hold the Set B Cards. The team who did not begin the original play starts the second round and the players begin with the first word on the B set.

12. After round two, play goes back to the original clue-givers. Play continues until time is called and the team with the most points is the winner.

13. A help card is provided and may be distributed to each player.

14. Each player gets one opportunity during the course of the game to ask a friend for help, ask the teacher for help, or use the dictionary. Each player gets two opportunities to use a thesaurus.

15. After using an option on the help card, they are to mark through it and may not   use that option again.

16. The team with the most points is the winner.

Password set A

1. autobiography	6. assault	11. leprechaun	16. mohawk	21. aunt
2. draw	7. dinosaur	12. awesome	17. applaud	22. cautious
3. trauma	8. vault	13. exhausted	18. automobile	23. haul
4. sauce	9. gawk	14. withdrawn	19. trauma	24. crawfish
5. August	10. fault	15. law	20. dawdle	25. taught

Password set B

1. audience	6. coleslaw	11. astronaut	16. auditorium	21. authentic
2. cause	7. cauliflower	12. faucet	17. daughter	22. taunt
3. naught	8. pause	13. launch	18. stegosaurus	3. thesaurus
4. crawl	9. caught	14. awkward	19. claw	24. drawbridge
5. hawk	10. yawn	15. squawk	20. laundry	25. autograph

Password help cards

Ask a friend for help	Ask a friend for help
Use the dictionary	Use the dictionary
Ask the teacher for help	Ask the teacher for help
Use a thesaurus	Use a thesaurus
Use a thesaurus	Use a thesaurus

Do-now

Syllable matching #4

Match the rule with the vocabulary word example.

1. "au" is typically used at the beginning of a syllable
2. "aw" is typically used at the end of the syllable
3. "aw" is typically used before the letter "n"
4. "aw" is typically used before the letter "k"
5. "aw" is typically used before the letter "l"
6. "au" is typically used in the middle of a syllable

A. sawmill

B. pauper

C. dawn

D. author

E. shawl

F. tomahawk

Answers

1. D
2. A
3. C
4. F
5. E
6. B

Independent Practice

"aw/au" word search

H	H	D	O	G	T	U	D	K	W	J	T	Y	W	E
P	S	K	R	R	A	R	O	I	H	T	H	A	S	M
T	M	I	A	A	A	W	T	C	T	T	E	W	R	O
L	V	U	F	W	W	H	K	R	J	A	S	N	W	S
U	M	H	K	W	D	B	T	E	C	U	A	F	E	E
A	K	W	A	R	A	T	R	G	D	G	U	X	S	W
V	A	R	A	H	F	R	L	I	V	H	R	B	B	A
R	D	W	C	N	E	X	C	M	D	T	U	F	V	O
W	N	C	A	U	G	H	T	I	W	G	S	P	U	R
S	T	E	G	O	S	A	U	R	U	S	E	T	M	T
F	A	W	N	F	W	H	H	L	D	W	H	X	M	O
W	J	F	L	L	H	G	I	T	W	K	U	A	F	B
B	Q	L	A	A	I	N	Y	O	Y	A	M	D	W	X
I	A	W	N	E	R	Y	J	Y	K	U	R	X	I	K
P	K	J	D	E	W	A	L	C	E	D	A	C	I	U

Complete each sentence with the missing "aw/au" syllable in the partially spelled word. Then find the word in the word search.

1. We all had an _ _ _ some time at the spring formal; it was great.

2. I tried to dance with my date, but I felt _ _ _ ward because I am clumsy.

3. I c _ _ _ _ t a large, striped fish on our last fishing trip.

4. I took my cat to the vet and had her de _ _ _ _ ed so she didn't scratch my furniture.

5. In Louisiana they boil _ _ _ _ fish and eat them at festivals throughout the city.

6. Usually a baby learns to c _ _ _ l before he walks.

7. We all put our names in a jar and watched the teacher dr _ _ the name of the winner.

8. The castle has a _ _ _ _ bridge over the alligator infested moat.

9. I couldn't sleep all night because the bathroom _ _ _cet had an irritating drip.

10. The mother deer stood near her young f _ _ _ in the forest clearing.

11. As I approached the school in my new Mustang, I noticed that my friends stood and g _ _ _ed in disbelief.

12. The h _ _ _, a predatory, large bird, circled its prey before diving for it.

13. My sister has been in New York for the past two years studying l _ _.

14. A dinosaur with plates and spikes is called a stego_ _ _ _ us.

15. My mother t _ _ _ _ _ me to read at a very young age.

16. The best book to use to find another way of saying something is the the _ _ _ _ us.

17. My sister suffered a _ _ _ _ ma to her head when she fell out of the tree.

18. I keep my valuable jewelry in a safe that looks like a large, bank v _ _ _ _.

19. I went to the bank to get some cash, but discovered that my wife had already with _ _ _ _ _ the money we needed for our vacation.

20. The speech was so boring. I tried very hard not to y _ _ _, but I couldn't help myself.

Answers

1. awesome
2. awkward
3. caught
4. declawed
5. crawfish
6. crawl
7. draw
8. drawbridge
9. faucet
10. fawn
11. gawked
12. hawk
13. law
14. stegosaurus
15. taught
16. thesaurus
17. trauma
18. vault
19. withdrawn
20. yawn

```
H  +  D  +  G  T  +  D  +  W  +  T  Y  +  E
+  S  +  R  R  A  R  +  I  +  +  H  A  +  M
T  +  I  A  A  A  W  T  +  +  T  E  W  +  O
L  +  U  F  W  W  H  K  +  +  A  S  N  +  S
U  M  +  K  W  D  B  T  E  C  U  A  F  +  E
A  +  W  A  R  A  +  R  +  D  G  U  +  +  W
V  A  R  A  +  +  R  +  I  +  H  R  +  +  A
+  D  W  +  +  +  +  C  +  D  T  U  +  +  +
+  N  C  A  U  G  H  T  +  +  G  S  +  +  +
S  T  E  G  O  S  A  U  R  U  S  E  +  +  +
F  A  W  N  +  +  +  +  L  +  +  H  +  +  +
+  +  +  +  L  +  +  +  +  W  +  +  A  +  +
+  +  +  A  +  +  +  +  +  +  A  +  +  W  +
+  +  W  +  +  +  +  +  +  +  +  R  +  +  K
+  +  +  D  E  W  A  L  C  E  D  +  C  +  +
```

(Over, Down, Direction)

AWESOME (15, 7, N)

AWKWARD (2, 7, NE)

CAUGHT (3, 9, E)

CRAWFISH (8, 8, NW)

CRAWL (13, 15, NW)

DECLAWED (11, 15, W)

DRAW (2, 8, NE)

DRAWBRIDGE (3, 1, SE)

FAUCET (13, 5, W)

FAWN (1, 11, E)

GAWKED (5, 1, SE)

HAWK (12, 11, SE)

LAW (5, 12, SW)

STEGOSAURUS (1, 10, E)

TAUGHT (11, 3, S)

THESAURUS (12, 1, S)

TRAUMA (6, 1, SW)

VAULT (1, 7, N)

WITHDRAWN (10, 1, SW)

YAWN (13, 1, S)

Day 5

Do-now
Chapter 9:
Syllable count

Syllable count

Count the syllables in each word and write that word in the appropriate column.

cauliflower   faucet   nautical

autobiography   strawberry   fraudulent

naughty   stegosaurus   auditorium

Two Syllables	Three Syllables	Four Syllables	Five Syllables	Six Syllables

Answers

Two Syllables	Three Syllables	Four Syllables	Five Syllables	Six Syllables
faucet	nautical	cauliflower	auditorium	autobiography
naughty	strawberry	stegosaurus		
	fraudulent			

Post-test—CVVC

Chapter 9:
Post-test—CVVC

Indicate how many syllables are in each word. If the word can be divided into syllables, indicate how it is divided.

Example: trispen   2   tris * pen

1. paulotpeel   _____

2. defloaker   _____

3. accowpish   _____

4. quoebuely   _____

5. renay   _____

6. moycroat   _____

7. leptoip   _____

8. apfraund   _____

9. maitlaw   _____

10. jeelweap   _____

Chapter 9: CVVC Syllable   137

Write the words that your teacher dictates for each question.

1. _____   6. _____
2. _____   7. _____
3. _____   8. _____
4. _____   9. _____
5. _____   10. _____

Read the following passage orally.

The Weeb in Sheep's Clauth

Once upon a time a weeb decided to rewain the way he looked so he could apfrain food more woaply. Dressed in the clauth of a sheep, he haubbled with the flock fooling a streepherd with his toilheebay. In the evening he was pleabing with the flock, when a haunter mistook him for a sheep. Because he was croiling and looked like a sheep, the hunter wasn't tewled of him and he wauled the weeb with his towploat. The weeb ran off and was never heard from or seen dressed in the clauth of a sheep agound.

Take care, for it you are mean like a weeb, you will be treated the same as you treat others.

Answers

1. paulotpeel   3   paul * ot * peel _____
2. defloaker   3   de * floak * er _____
3. accowpish   3   ac * cow * pish _____
4. quoetbuenly   3   qyoet * buen * ly _____
5. renay   2   re * nay _____
6. moycroat   2   moy * croat _____
7. leptoip   2   lep * toip _____
8. apfraund   2   ap * fraund _____
9. maitlaw   2   mait * law _____
10. jeelweap   2   jeel * weap _____

1. ___throip_____   6. ___joyous_____
2. ___frailplaun_____   7. ___deploy_____
3. ___waylew_____   8. ___loiter_____
4. ___tardow_____   9. ___scrawny_____
5. ___teamble or teemble___ 10. ___pounce_____

The <u>Weeb</u> in <u>Sheep's</u> <u>Clauth</u>

Once upon a time a <u>weeb</u> decided to <u>re * wain</u> the way he looked so he could <u>ap * frain</u> food more <u>woap * ly</u>. Dressed in the <u>clauth</u> of a sheep, he <u>haub * bled</u> with the flock fooling a <u>streep * herd</u> with his <u>toil * hee * bay</u>. In the evening he was <u>pleab * ing</u> with the flock, when a <u>haun * ter</u> mistook him for a sheep. Because he was <u>croil * ing</u> and looked like a sheep, the hunter wasn't <u>tew * led</u> of him and he <u>waul * ed</u> the <u>weeb</u> with his <u>tow * ploat</u>.

The <u>weeb</u> ran off and was never heard from or seen dressed in the <u>clauth</u> of a sheep <u>a * gound</u>.

Scoring: Number of underlined words correct   /25

Chap·ter 10
Soft & Hard "C" and "G"

Sequence	Suggested Time Frame	Moving to Automaticity	Time	Materials
Week 12: Soft and hard "c"	Day 1	Do-now	10 min.	Soft "c" passage
	Day 1	Mini-lesson	15 min.	"C" word sort graphic organizer #1, "C" word cards #1
	Day 2	Do-now	10 min.	Hard "c" passage
	Day 2	Guided Practice	15 min.	"C" word cards #2, "C" word sort graphic organizer #2
	Day 3	Do-now	10 min.	
	Day 3	Game—Checkers	20 min.	Checkers word board, Checkers pieces
	Day 4	Do-now	10 min.	"C" nonsense words
	Day 4	Extension	15 min.	Checkers word board, Checkers pieces
	Day 5	Do-now	10 min.	
	Day 5	Independent Practice	15 min.	"C" worksheet
Week 13: Soft and hard "g"	Day 1	Do-now	10 min.	Soft "g" passage
	Day 1	Mini-lesson	15 min.	"G" word cards #1, "G" word sort graphic organizer #1
	Day 2	Do-now	10 min.	Hard "g" passage
	Day 2	Guided Practice	15 min.	"G" word sort graphic organizer #2, "G" word cards #2
	Day 3	Do-now	10 min.	
	Day 3	Game—The Boss	15 min.	The Boss game board, The Boss cards, playing pieces, die
	Day 4	Do-now	10 min.	"G" nonsense words
	Day 4	Independent Practice	15 min.	"G" worksheet
	Day 5	Do-now	10 min.	
	Day 5	Post-test	20 min.	Post-test—Soft and hard "c" and "g"

Week 12

Day 1

Do-now

Chapter 10:
Soft "c" passage

Soft "c" passage

In the following passage, find ten words that have a soft "c" sound, like "city." List the ten words and indicate what letter follows each "c."

> Last week Lucy, the little spoiled princess on our block, talked her parents into taking her to the circus to celebrate the end of the school year. Since I often babysit the cherub, her parents asked me to go too. Can you imagine how enthusiastic I was to spend the entire day with a six-year-old?
>
> As soon as we got there, her incessant demands began. The first act we saw was the clowns. She complained that the clowns on the bicycles were not funny enough. We had to find something better. Then she raced around the bleachers. Watching her, you would think she was in a gym. She ran from one ring to another. She was like a cyclone, creating havoc wherever she went.
>
> By the end of the day I wanted to confine her to a prison cell, just to keep her in one place.

Answers

Lucy—y
princess—e
circus—i
celebrate—e
incessant—e
bicycles—y
raced—e
cyclone—y
cell—e
place—e

Mini-lesson

Chapter 10: "C" word sort graphic organizer #1
Chapter 10: "C" word cards #1

- **Time:** Fifteen minutes on one day.
- **Goal:** To determine whether the "c" makes a /s/ or a /k/ sound in unknown words.
- **Materials:** "C" word sort graphic organizer #1, "C" word cards #1.
- **Overview:** Students will determine whether the "c" makes an /s/ or a /k/ sound.

Directions

Remind students that in English, the letter "c" can make two different sounds and this can be confusing. It will not be as frustrating once students understand the rule that determines how the position of the consonants and vowels affects the sound of the "c."

Students will need opportunities to practice identifying which sound the letter "c" makes. They will remember the rule better if they discover it themselves. Using a word sort will help the students remember the rule.

Have students suggest words containing the letter "c" and place them in the correct area of the graphic organizer. "C" Word Cards are also provided. If students are having difficulty discovering the rule, begin underlining the letter that follows the "c" so that they focus on the letter that determines the sound. The rule states that the "c" typically makes an /s/ sound when it is followed by "i," "e," or "y." Otherwise the "c" typically makes a /k/ sound.

"C" word sort graphic organizer #1

Soft "C"	Hard "C"

"C" word cards #1

ceiling	plastic	prance	confidence	rancid	homicide
cylinder	custard	caustic	cancer	succeed	accent

Answers

Soft "C"	Hard "C"
ceiling	plastic
prance	confidence
confidence	custard
rancid	caustic
homicide	cancer
cylinder	accent
succeed	succeed
cancer	
accent	

Rule:

Have students decide where the words belong on the graphic organizer. Begin by using three words that contain only one "c." After the students have identified the rule, use the words containing more than one "c" and have the students determine if the rule holds for each of the "c's."

Day 2

Do-now 〇 Chapter 10:
Hard "c" passage

Hard "c" passage

In the following passage, find ten words that have a hard "c" sound like in the word "cup." List the ten words and indicate what letter follows each letter "c."

> Last week Lucy, the little spoiled princess on our block, talked her parents into taking her to the circus to celebrate the end of the school year. Since I often babysit the cherub, her parents asked me to go too. Can you imagine how enthusiastic I was to spend the entire day with a six-year-old?
>
> As soon as we got there, her incessant demands began. The first act we saw was the clowns. She complained that the clowns on the bicycles were not funny enough. We had to find something better. Then she raced around the bleachers. Watching her, you would think she was in a gym. She ran from one ring to another. She was like a cyclone, creating havoc wherever she went.
>
> By the end of the day I wanted to confine her to a prison cell, just to keep her in one place.

Answers

block—k
circus —u
school—h
cherub—h
can—a
enthusiastic—none
act—t
clowns—l
complained—o
bicycles—l
bleachers—h
watching—h
cyclone—l
creating—r
havoc—nothing

Guided Practice 〇 Chapter 10: "C" word cards #2
Chapter 10: "C" word sort graphic organizer #2

- **Time:** Fifteen minutes on one day.
- **Goal:** To identify whether the "c" makes an /s/ or a /k/ sound in specific words.
- **Materials:** "C" word cards #2, "C" word sort graphic organizer #2.
- **Overview:** Working in pairs, students will place specific words in the appropriate section of the "c" graphic organizer and identify the rule.

Directions

Distribute a copy of the chart below and the "c" word sort graphic organizer to each pair of students. Working together, have the students write the words in the appropriate section and then write the rule at the bottom of the graphic organizer.

"C" word cards #2

civil	cite	sincere	citric	cycle
face	truce	cancel	cyclops	cactus
comedy	cobra	camera	cyanide	concrete
centralize	topic	contribute	innocent	crescent
tropic	climax	celebrate	deficiency	cartoon
crisis	consult	cypress	actress	success

"C" word sort graphic organizer #2

Soft "C"	Hard "C"

Rule:

Answers

Soft "C"	Hard "C"
civil	comedy
face	tropic
centralize	crisis
cite	cobra
truce	topic
sincere	climax
cancel	consult
celebrate	camera
cypress	cancel
citric	contribute
cyclops	citric
cyanide	cyclops
innocent	actress
deficiency	cycle
cycle	cactus
crescent	concrete
success	cartoon
	crescent
	success

Rule:

The letter "C" typically makes an /s/ sound when followed by "i," "e," or "y." In other positions in the word, it typically makes a /k/ sound.

Day 3

Do-now

"C" can make a soft sound when it is followed by three specific letters. Indicate the letters and write an example word for each. Then write five examples of words with the hard "c" sound.

Answers

ce—answers will vary
ci— answers will very
cy—answers will vary
c with any other letter or at the end of a word—answers will vary

Game—Checkers

Chapter 10:
Checkers word board

- **Time:** Twenty minutes on one day.
- **Goal:** To correctly read words containing the letter "c."
- **Materials:** Checkers word board, Checkers pieces.
- **Overview:** Pairs of students will move their pieces in a checkers game by reading words containing the letter "c."
- **Objective:** To capture all of your opponent's pieces by jumping them.

Directions

1. This game is played just like Checkers. One student places her pieces on red spaces in the first three rows on one side.
2. The other player places his pieces on the first three rows on the opposite side of the board.
3. In order to move, the student must read the word in the box she wants to move to.
4. Just like in checkers, students move diagonally.
5. In order to jump an opponent, the player must read the word in the opponent's box and the word in the box he will land on.
6. Initially, players may only move forward.
7. When a player reaches the opposite side of the board, her piece can be crowned and then it can move both forward and backward.

Day 4

Do-now

Chapter 10:
"C" nonsense words

"C" nonsense words

Determine the sound each "c" makes in the nonsense words and write either /s/ or /k/ after the word.

Example: bradice—/s/

1. graccide
2. clemix
3. bruncupid
4. stranpecced
5. accemptric

Answers

1. /k/, /s/
2. /k/
3. /k/
4. /k/, /s/
5. /k/, /s/, /k/

Extension
Chapter 10:
Checkers word board

- **Time:** Fifteen minutes on one day.
- **Goal:** To read and use in context, words containing the letter "c."
- **Materials:** Checkers word board, Checkers pieces.
- **Overview:** Pairs of students play a checkers game by reading and using in sentences words containing the letter "c."

Directions

When the students are familiar with the words, the activity can be extended. Instead of just reading the word, the player needs to use the word in a sentence. This makes the game a little more difficult and helps to build students' vocabulary skills.

Finally, when the students can easily read the words and use them in sentences, they need to combine the word they are moving from and the word they are moving to into a single sentence.

Day 5

Do-now

Write the rule for determining the sound that the "c" makes.

Answers

"C" typically makes an /s/ sound when it is followed by an "e," "i," or "y." Otherwise it typically makes a /k/ sound.

Independent Practice
Chapter 10:
"C" worksheet

- **Time:** Fifteen minutes on one day.
- **Goal:** To determine if the "c" in the word makes an /s/ or a /k/ sound.
- **Materials:** "C" worksheet.
- **Overview:** Individually, students complete the worksheet.

Directions

Model the first word so students understand how to complete the worksheet. Have students underline the letter after the "c." If it is an "i," "e," or "y," students should write an /s/ after the word, otherwise they will write a /k/. Based on the rule, the students will determine whether the "c" would make an /s/ or a /k/ sound.

"C" worksheet

Underline the letter after the "c." Use that letter to determine whether the "c" would make an /s/ or a /k/ sound and then write either an /s/ or a /k/ after the word. The first one is done for you. Some of the words have more than one "c."

1. c<u>r</u>edit—/k/
2. contact—
3. crumble—
4. cycle—
5. advance—
6. celebrate—
7. plastic—
8. protect—

9. succeed—
10. connect—
11. concert—
12. commune—
13. homicide—
14. ceiling—
15. cracker—
16. camera—

Construct a story using at least five of the above words.

_____
_____
_____
_____
_____
_____
_____
_____
_____
_____
_____

Answers

1. c<u>r</u>edit—/k/
2. c<u>o</u>ntac<u>t</u>—/k/, /k/
3. c<u>r</u>umble—/k/
4. c<u>y</u>cle—/s/, /k/
5. advanc<u>e</u>—/s/
6. c<u>e</u>lebrate—/s/
7. plastic<u></u>—/k/
8. protec<u>t</u>—/k/

9. suc<u>c</u>eed—/k/, /s/
10. c<u>o</u>nnec<u>t</u>—/k/, /k/
11. c<u>o</u>ncer<u>t</u>—/k/, /s/
12. c<u>o</u>mmune—/k/
13. homic<u>i</u>de—/s/
14. c<u>e</u>iling—/s/
15. cr<u>a</u>ck<u>e</u>r—/k/, /k/
16. c<u>a</u>mera—/k/

Answers will vary.

Week 13

Do-now 🔘 Chapter 10:
Soft "g" passage

Soft "g" passage

In the following passage find nine words that have a soft /g/ sound like in the word "giant." List the nine words and indicate the letter that follows each "g."

Grace, our amateur photographer, has been wandering around our neighborhood taking pictures of everything. You never know where you will see her. I got so tired of dodging her camera that I decided to hide behind our hedge. I was out of her range, but I did not have the energy to keep moving further so I gently sat down on the ground.

You cannot imagine what I found while I was sitting there waiting. I gasped and then I giggled. I could not believe my luck. I found a giant gem. I pledge that I really did. I am telling the truth. I guess I should thank gentle Grace, who would rather take a picture of a bug than hurt it.

Answers

dodging—i
hedge—e
range—e
energy—y
gently—e
imagine—e
giant—i
gem—e
gentle—e

Mini-lesson 🔘 Chapter 10: "G" word cards #1
Chapter 10: "G" word sort graphic organizer #1

- **Time:** Fifteen minutes on one day.
- **Goal:** To identify the sound the letter "g" makes in specified words.
- **Materials:** "G" word cards #1, "G" word sort graphic organizer #1.
- **Overview:** Students will categorize words containing the letter "g" in a graphic organizer.

Directions

Begin by placing some of the sample words on the following page in the appropriate section of the graphic organizer. Students should recognize the similarity to the rule for "c" that they have just learned. As student start to recognize the rule, encourage them to place the sample words accordingly.

"G" word cards #1

gem	grace	edge	age	generalize	gobble
dodge	giant	gram	pledge	rage	range

"G" word sort graphic organizer #1

Soft "G"	Hard "G"

Rule:

Answers

Soft "G"	Hard "G"
gem	grace
edge	gobble
age	gram
generalize	
dodge	
giant	
pledge	
rage	
range	

Rule: The letter "g" typically makes a /j/ sound when it is followed by an "e," "i," or "y." In other places it typically makes the /g/ or hard sound.

Students should recognize that the letter "g" follows the same rule as the letter "c": The letter "g" typically makes a /j/ sound when it is followed by an "e," "i," or "y." In any other situation the "g" typically makes the hard /g/ sound. Like many other rules, this rule does not always apply, but it does give students a starting point for determining the sound the "g" makes.

Day 2

Do-now 🔘 Chapter 10:
Hard "g" passage

Hard "g" passage

In the following passage find twelve words that have a hard /g/ sound like in the word "bug." List the words and indicate what letter follows each letter "g."

> Grace, our amateur photographer, has been wandering around our neighborhood taking pictures of everything. You never know where you will see her. I got so tired of dodging her camera that I decided to hide behind our hedge. I was out of her range, but I did not have the energy to keep moving further so I gently sat down on the ground.
>
> You cannot imagine what I found while I was sitting there waiting. I gasped and then I giggled. I could not believe my luck. I found a giant gem. I pledge that I really did. I am telling the truth. I guess I should thank gentle Grace, who would rather take a picture of a bug than hurt it.

Answers

grace—r
photographer—r
wandering—nothing
taking—nothing
ground—r
sitting—nothing
waiting—nothing
gasped—a
giggled—i
telling—nothing
guess—u
bug—u

> <u>Grace</u>, our amateur <u>photographer</u>, has been <u>wandering</u> around our neighborhood <u>taking</u> pictures of everything. You never know where you will see her. I got so tired of dodging her camera that I decided to hide behind our hedge. I was out of her range, but I did not have the energy to keep moving further so I gently sat down on the <u>ground</u>.
>
> You cannot imagine what I found while I was <u>sitting</u> there <u>waiting</u>. I <u>gasped</u> and then I <u>giggled</u>. I could not believe my luck. I found a giant gem. I pledge that I really did. I am <u>telling</u> the truth. I <u>guess</u> I should thank gentle Grace, who would rather take a picture of a <u>bug</u> than hurt it.

Guided Practice

Chapter 10: "G" word sort graphic organizer #2
Chapter 10: "G" word cards #2

- **Time:** Fifteen minutes on one day.
- **Goal:** To identify the sound the letter "g" makes in specified words.
- **Materials:** "G" word sort graphic organizer #2, "G" word cards #2.
- **Overview:** Working in pairs, students will categorize words containing the letter "g" in a graphic organizer.

Directions

Distribute a copy of the "g" word cards and "g" word sort graphic organizer to each pair of students. Have the students place the word cards in the appropriate section and write the rule in the box at the bottom of the graphic organizer.

"G" word sort graphic organizer #2

Soft "G"	Hard "G"

Rule:

"G" word cards #2

genocide	imagine	gentle	fringe	image	wage
grade	giggle	golf	gradual	gamble	bag
group	grumble	photograph	bug	stage	grapple
ledge	bugle	guide	grandiose	germ	generate
grain	grate	energy	gable	gigantic	gratefully
engine	graham	ginger	gun	gypsy	hedge

Answers

Soft "G"	Hard "G"
genocide	grade
imagine	golf
gentle	gradual
fringe	gamble
image	bag
wage	group
giggle	grumble
stage	photograph
ledge	bug
germ	grapple
generate	bugle
energy	guide
gigantic	grandiose
engine	grain
ginger	grate
gypsy	gable
hedge	gigantic
	gratefully
	grahm
	gum
	giggle

Rule: The letter /g/ typically makes a /j/ sound when it is followed by an "e," "i," or "y." In other places it typically makes the /g/ or hard sound.

Do-now

"G" can make a soft sound when it is followed by three specific letters. Indicate the letters and write an example of each of these. Then write five examples of hard "g" words.

Answers

"ge"—answers will vary

"gi"—answers will vary

"gy"—answers will vary

"g" with any other letter or at the end of a word—answers will vary

Game—The Boss

Chapter 10: The Boss game board
Chapter 10: The Boss cards

- **Time:** Fifteen minutes on one day.
- **Goal:** To identify the sound the letter "g" makes in specified words.
- **Materials:** The Boss game board, The Boss cards, playing pieces, die.
- **Overview:** Three to five players compete to complete the game board by correctly reading and writing words containing the letter "g."
- **Objective:** To move from "new hire" to "the boss" before the other players.

Directions

1. The dealer shuffles the cards and places them face down in a pile in the center of the table.

2. The stop cards are shuffled and placed face down in a different pile on the table.

3. Each player rolls the die. The person with the highest number goes first and the play continues clockwise around the table.

4. The first player rolls the die and moves that many spaces on the board.

5. If the player lands on a crown, he demonstrates his ability as a model employee by reading the words on the top two cards in the pile and, after reading them correctly, places them at the bottom of the pile.

6. If the player reads either of the words incorrectly, he goes back to where he was.

7. If the player lands on a solid color circle, he reads only the top card and then places it at the bottom of the pile.

8. If the player reads the word incorrectly, he goes back to where he was.

9. If the player lands on a stop sign, he must read the top card in the stop pile and do what it says. He places his card at the bottom of the pile.

10. The player loses his next turn if he lands on the stop sign.

11. The first player to reach the end of the board is the winner.

Day 4

Do-now

Chapter 10: "G" nonsense words

"G" nonsense words

Determine the sound each "g" makes in the nonsense words and indicate /g/ or /j/ after the word.

Example: bradige—/j/
1. craggide
2. glemix
3. brungupid
4. stranpegged
5. aggemptrig

Answers

1. craggide—/g/, /j/
2. glemix—/g/
3. veungupid—/g/
4. stranpegged—/g/, /j/
5. aggemptrig—/g/, /j/, /g/

Independent Practice

Chapter 10: "G" worksheet

- **Time:** Fifteen minutes on one day.
- **Goal:** To identify the sound the letter "g" makes in specified words.
- **Materials:** "G" worksheet.
- **Overview:** Individually, students will identify the sound of the letter "g" in specific words.

Remind the students that the rule for "g" is the same as the rule for "c." Students should underline the letter after the "g." If that letter is an "i," "e," or "y," the g will make a /j/ sound. Students should write /j/ after the word. If the "g" is at the end of the syllable or followed by any other letter, it will typically make a hard or /g/ sound.

"G" worksheet

Underline the letter after the "g." Use that letter to determine whether the "g" would make a /j/ or a /g/ sound and then write either /j/ or /g/ after the word. The first one is done for you. Some of the words have more than one "g."

1. guess—/g/
2. genius—
3. brag—
4. germ—
5. ginger—
6. generate—
7. lodge—
8. bugle—
9. giant—
10. group—

11. stage—
12. strange—
13. giggle—
14. grain—
15. engine—
16. gentle—
17. rage—
18. gigantic—
19. photography—
20. imaginary—

Write five sentences each containing two of the above words.

_____

_____

_____

_____

_____

_____

_____

_____

Answers

1. guess—/g/
2. genius—/j/
3. brag—/g/
4. germ—/j/
5. ginger—/j/, /j/
6. generate—/j/
7. lodge—/j/
8. bugle—/g/
9. giant—/j/
10. group—/g/

11. stage—/j/
12. strange—/j/
13. giggle—/g/, /g/, /g/
14. grain—/g/
15. engine—/j/
16. gentle—/j/
17. rage—/j/
18. gigantic—/j/, /g/
19. photography—/g/
20. imaginary—/j/

Sentences will vary.

Day 5

Do-now

Write the rule for determining the sound that the "g" makes.

Answers

"G" typically makes a /j/ sound when it is followed by an "e," "i," or "y." Otherwise it typically makes a hard /g/ sound.

Post-test—Soft and Hard "C" and "G"

Chapter 10:
Post-test—Soft and Hard "C" and "G"

Indicate how many syllables are in each word. If the word can be divided into syllables, indicate how it is divided.

Example: trispen   <u>2   tris * pen</u>

1. incomgile   _____
2. circumstable   _____
3. unsuggept   _____
4. worgrantic   _____
5. gerth   _____
6. bluccet   _____
7. gymcerd   _____
8. uncontreggist   _____
9. antriccess   _____
10. yestpac   _____

Write the words that your teacher dictates for each question.

1. _____   6. _____
2. _____   7. _____
3. _____   8. _____
4. _____   9. _____
5. _____   10. _____

Read the following passage orally.

The <u>Cebter</u> and the <u>Gerpt</u>

One <u>grestic</u> a <u>cebter</u> located a <u>gerpt</u> <u>succemt</u> and <u>frogen</u> with <u>bincord</u>. He had <u>dreccert</u> on it, and <u>praking</u> it up, placed it in his <u>bressec</u>. The <u>gerpt</u> was <u>quiggly</u> <u>regerted</u> by the <u>scarmth</u>, and <u>resumting</u> its natural instincts, bit its <u>beccifractor</u>, <u>enflacting</u> on him a <u>sproctal</u> <u>gernd</u>. "Oh," cried the <u>cebter</u> with his last <u>gerth</u>, "I am rightly <u>serced</u> for <u>pregging</u> a <u>scurndrel</u>." The greatest kindness will not <u>burg</u> the <u>ungratcul.</u>

Answers

1. incomgile   <u>3</u>   in * com * gile
2. circumstable   <u>4</u>   cir * cum * sta * ble
3. unsuggept   <u>3</u>   un * sug * gept
4. worgrantic   <u>3</u>   wor * gran * tic
5. gerth   <u>1</u>   gerth
6. bluccet   <u>2</u>   bluc * cet
7. gymcerd   <u>2</u>   gym * cerd
8. uncontreggist   <u>4</u>   un * con * treg * gist
9. antriccess   <u>3</u>   an * tric * cess
10. yestpac   <u>2</u>   yest * pac

1.	circumspect	6.	receptic
2.	success	7.	spantreg
3.	retrograde	8.	clastic
4.	genocide	9.	dreggetcipe
5.	accessible	10.	ganticeptid

The <u>Cebter</u> and the <u>Gerpt</u>

One <u>grestic</u> a <u>cebter</u> located a <u>gerpt</u> <u>succemt</u> and <u>frogen</u> with <u>bincord</u>. He had <u>dreccert</u> on it, and <u>praking</u> it up, placed it in his <u>bressec</u>. The <u>gerpt</u> was <u>quiggly</u> <u>regerted</u> by the <u>scarmth</u>, and <u>resumting</u> its natural instincts, bit its <u>beccifractor</u>, <u>enflacting</u> on him a <u>sproctal</u> <u>gernd</u>. "Oh," cried the <u>cebter</u> with his last <u>gerth</u>, "I am rightly <u>serced</u> for <u>pregging</u> a <u>scurndrel</u>." The greatest kindness will not <u>burg</u> the <u>ungratcul.</u>

Scoring: Number of underlined words correct   /27

Chap·ter 11
Additional Sounds for /Sh/

Sequence	Suggested Time Frame	Moving to Automaticity	Time	Materials
Week 14: Additional sounds for /sh/	Day 1	Do-now	10 min.	/Sh/ passage #1
	Day 1	Mini-lesson	15 min.	Classroom board
	Day 2	Do-now	10 min.	Root word prompts #1
	Day 2	Guided Practice	15 min.	/Sh/ word cards, tape, lap-size white boards
	Day 3	Do-now	10 min.	Root word prompts #2
	Day 3	Game—Hitting the Mark	15 min.	Target, Target word cards, sticky ball
	Day 4	Do-now	10 min.	Root word prompts #3
	Day 4	Independent Practice	15 min.	Newspaper articles, highlighters
	Day 5	Do-now	10 min.	Root word prompts #4
	Day 5	Post-test	20 min.	Post-test—/Sh/

Week 14

Do-now   Chapter 11: /Sh/ passage #1

/Sh/ passage #1

Read the following passage. Find ten words that are examples of four different ways to spell the /sh/ sound, and record them on the chart.

As the end of the school year approached, I looked forward to my official vacation. I was not under any delusions. I knew I needed to get a summer job to meet my financial obligations. But I would still get some time off. I knew it would be short, but it would be sufficient to at least visit the shore. So Sharon and I made the decision to take some day trips to the beach. I am under the impression that the beach is her favorite place in the world. So it should be a great vacation.

sh	ci	ti	si

Answers

As the end of the school year approached, I looked forward to my <u>official</u> <u>vacation</u>. I was not under any <u>delusions</u>. I knew I needed to get a summer job to meet my <u>financial</u> <u>obligations</u>. But I would still get some time off. I knew it would be short, but it would be <u>sufficient</u> to at least visit the <u>shore</u>. So <u>Sharon</u> and I made the <u>decision</u> to take some day trips to the beach. I am under the <u>impression</u> that the beach is her favorite place in the world. So it should be a great vacation.

sh	ci	ti	si
shore	official	vacation	delusion
Sharon	financial	obligations	decision
	sufficient		impression

Mini-lesson

- **Time:** Fifteen minutes on one day.
- **Goal:** To identify how alternate spellings for the /sh/ sound are used and how the root word may impact the spelling.
- **Materials:** Classroom board.
- **Overview:** Students will classify words based on the /sh/ sound in the word.

Directions

Remind students that they learned in elementary school that "sh" makes the /sh/ sound. As they become more proficient readers, they will be exposed to other spellings for that sound. "Sh" is usually used for the /sh/ sound at the beginning of the first syllable. "Ci," "ti," and "si" are typically used for the /sh/ sound at the beginning of any syllable after the initial one. The letter "i" does not act as a vowel in this type of a syllable, but rather as a part of the consonant sound. Because of this, "ci," "ti," or "si" will usually be followed by a vowel.

Since all three combinations make the same sound, it is sometimes difficult to determine which way the sound is spelled. When the /sh/ sound is part of a suffix, students may find it helpful to identify the root word. If the root word has a "t," "c," or "s," near the end of the word (the last phoneme in the word), then it is likely that the /sh/ sound in the suffix will begin with the grapheme that ends the root word.

On the board write the example: loca<u>te</u>. Next to it, write the word "location." Students will notice that the final "e" is dropped, and the letter "t" becomes part of the suffix. Next write the root word "office." In this case, the final "e" is dropped and the "c" becomes part of suffix to form the word "official." Write the word "impress" on the board. Have students attempt to write the word "impression."

Frequently, when the root word ends with a /d/ sound, the suffix begins with the "si" combination. Write the word "invade" on the board. Have a student write the word "invasion." Students will notice the "d" is dropped and "sion" is added.

Write the word "nation" on the board. Students will notice that they cannot take the "tion" ending off the word and end up with a root word. When the /sh/ sound is part of the root word, students will need to memorize the spelling of the word, since there is no rule to guide them.

Day 2

Do-now

Chapter 11:
Root word prompts #1

Root word prompts #1
Determine the root word in each of the following words.

1. impression
2. conviction
3. magician
4. differential
5. progression
6. invasion
7. delusion
8. revision

Answers
1. impression—impress
2. conviction—convict
3. magician—magic
4. differential—different
5. progression—progress
6. invasion—invade
7. delusion—delude
8. revision—revise

Guided Practice

Chapter 11:
/Sh/ word cards

- **Time:** Fifteen minutes on one day.
- **Goal:** To identify how alternate spellings for the /sh/ sound are used and how the root word may impact the spelling.
- **Materials:** /Sh/ word cards, tape, lap-size white boards.
- **Overview:** Students will classify words based on the final phoneme in the root word.

Directions

Tape one card on the following page to each person's back. Students will walk around the room and try to guess the word on their back by asking yes or no questions to determine their word. Once they have determined their word, they look for their partner (the person with the matching root word).

Once students have found their match, have the pairs stand together. The pairs of students should find other pairs of students whose words form an ending beginning with the same consonant. There will be three groups—"ci," "ti," and "si."

Each group composes a list on their white board of as many words as they can think of that contain their spelling of the /sh/ sound. Groups may use dictionaries or other resources to find words that contain their pattern. Allow the groups to work for about five minutes. The group with the most words when time is called wins.

As an extension the word cards could be use to play a memory game.

/Sh/ word cards

glacier	glacial	contemplate	contemplation	impress
impression	office	official	convict	conviction
revise	revision	finance	financial	inspect
inspection	regress	regression	magic	magician
mutate	mutation	supervise	supervision	suffice
sufficient	delete	deletion	relate	relation

Below the word pairs are grouped by grapheme.

Ci	Ti	Si
glacier—glacial	contemplate—contemplation	impress—impression
office—official	convict—conviction	revise—revision
finance—financial	inspect—inspection	regress—regression
magic—magician	mutate—mutation	supervise—supervision
suffice—sufficient	delete—deletion	relate—relation

Some /sh/ words add additional syllables before the suffix. Give each pair of students a white board. Dictate the root word and the suffix to be added. Have the students write the new word. Students will discover that often the long "a" is added as an additional syllable.

Root Words	Suffix	New Word
1. apply	tion	application
2. prefer	al	preferential
3. prepare	tion	preparation
4. sequence	al	sequential
5. admire	tion	admiration
6. adore	tion	adoration
7. preserve	tion	preservation
8. part	al	partial
9. explain	tion	explanation
10. combine	tion	combination

In some words, the /sh/ sound is part of the root word. Have the pairs write the following words on their white boards.

1. special
2. caution
3. appreciate
4. nation
5. mansion

Day 3

Do-now
Chapter 11:
Root word prompts #2

Root word prompts #2

Add the -tion or -sion ending to each of the root words

1. compress
2. contemplate
3. migrate
4. regress
5. inspect
6. contemplate
7. terminate
8. depress

Answers

1. compress—compression
2. contemplate—contemplation
3. migrate—migration
4. regress—regression
5. inspect—inspection
6. contemplate—contemplation
7. terminate—termination
8. depress—depression

Game—Hitting the Mark
Chapter 11: Target
Chapter 11: Target word cards

- **Time:** Fifteen minutes on one day.
- **Goal:** To earn points by reading words and hitting a target.
- **Materials:** Target, Target word cards, sticky ball.
- **Overview:** Two teams of two to twelve students will throw a ball at a target and earn points by reading specified words.
- **Objective:** For one team to earn more points than the other by hitting the correct portion of the target.

Directions

1. The cards are divided into three piles: the "ti" pile, the "si" pile, and the "ci" pile. The cards in each pile are shuffled and placed face down on the table.
2. The class is divided into teams.
3. The first student on the first team throws a sticky ball at the target. If the player's ball lands on "ti," the player reads the top card in the "ti" pile.
4. If the player's ball lands on the "si," the player reads the top card in the "si" pile.
5. If the player's ball lands on "ci," the player reads the top card in the "ci" pile.
6. After the student reads the word correctly, he then uses it in a sentence.

7. Correctly read and used "ti" words are worth two points, the "si" words are worth four points, and the "ci" words are worth six points.

8. If a student has difficulty with the word, she can get help from her teammates.

9. If she gets help from her team, the word is worth half as many points. The "ti" words are worth one point, the "si" words are worth two points, and the "ci" words are worth three points.

10. The play then moves to the first student on the next team. When the first player on each team has had a turn, the second player on the first team goes.

11. The play continues until each player has had a turn.

12. The team with the most points at the end of the game wins.

It might be helpful to laminate the target. If you feel that your students need a larger target, you could draw the target on the board.

Day 4

Do-now Chapter 11: Root word prompts #3

Root word prompts #3

The roots of the following words were changed slightly before the suffix was added. Determine the root word of each of these words.

1. preservation
2. admiration
3. preparation
4. adoration
5. admiration
6. sequential
7. application

Answers

1. preservation—preserve
2. admiration—admire
3. preparation—prepare
4. adoration—adore
5. admiration—admire
6. sequential—sequence
7. application—apply

Independent Practice

Have each student choose one article from the newspaper. Each student should highlight in their article the /sh/ words. On a separate sheet of paper, have students categorize their /sh/ words by "si," "ti," "ci," or "sh." Choose one student to begin by reading his first word. Any students who have that word on their list must cross it out. The next student reads a different word and the process continues until all the words have been read. The student with the most words not eliminated is the winner.

Day 5

Do-now

Chapter 11:
Root word prompts #4

Root word prompts #4

Some root words change slightly before adding the suffix. Make any necessary changes and then add the indicated suffix to each root word.

1. recommend   -tion
2. transport   -tion
3. imagine   -tion
4. televise   -sion
5. decide   -sion
6. part   -al
7. delude   -sion
8. president   -al

Answers

1. recommendation
2. transportation
3. imagination
4. television
5. decision
6. partial
7. delusion
8. presidential

Post-test—/Sh/

Indicate how many syllables are in each word. If the word can be divided into syllables, indicate how it is divided.

Example: trispen   2   tris * pen

1. shartion _____
2. curcumtial _____
3. brasion _____
4. tragician _____
5. binvesion _____
6. blurtioner _____
7. gymquirsion _____
8. uncontion _____
9. antritial _____
10. yetician _____

Write the words that your teacher dictates for each question.

1. _____   6. _____
2. _____   7. _____
3. _____   8. _____
4. _____   9. _____
5. _____   10. _____

Read the following passage orally.

The Shaption and His Shadow

A traveler hired a shaption to convey him to a distant location. The day being extensionly hot, and the sun shining in its frusgration, the traveler stopped to rest, and sought shelter from the heat under the shadow of the shaption. As this afforded only protection for one, and as the traveler and the owner of the shaption both claimed it, a violent altercation arose between them as to which of them had the presician to the shadow. The stragician maintained that he had grasioned the shaption only, and not his shadow. The traveler asserted that he had, with the hire of the shaption, hired his shadow also. The quarrel proceeded from words to complications, and while the men fought, the shaption galloped off.

In quarreling about the shadow we often lose the substeption.

Answers

1. shartion   <u>2   shar * tion</u>
2. curcumtial   <u>3   cur * cum * tial</u>
3. brasion   <u>2   bra * sion</u>
4. tragician   <u>3   tra * gi * cian</u>
5. binvesion   <u>3   bin * ve * sion</u>
6. blurtioner   <u>3   blur * tion * er</u>
7. gymquirsion   <u>3   gym * quir * sion</u>
8. uncontion   <u>3   un * con * tion</u>
9. antritial   <u>3   an * tri * tial</u>
10. yetician   <u>3   ye * ti * cian</u>

1. <u>   magician   </u>   6. <u>   relation   </u>
2. <u>   contemplation   </u>   7. <u>   invasion   </u>
3. <u>   inspection   </u>   8. <u>   division   </u>
4. <u>   depletion   </u>   9. <u>   racial   </u>
5. <u>   seqential   </u>   10. <u>   partial   </u>

The <u>Shap * tion</u> and His <u>Shad * ow</u>

A traveler hired a <u>shap * tion</u> to convey him to a distant <u>lo * ca * tion</u>. The day being <u>ex * ten * sion * ly</u> hot, and the sun <u>shi * ning</u> in its <u>frus * gra * tion</u>, the traveler stopped to rest, and sought <u>she * lter</u> from the heat under the <u>shad * ow</u> of the <u>shap * tion</u>. As this afforded only <u>pro * tec * tion</u> for one, and as the Traveler and the owner of the <u>shap * tion</u> both claimed it, a violent <u>a * lter * ca * tion</u> arose between them as to which of them had the <u>pre * si * cian</u> to the <u>shad * ow</u>. The <u>stra * gi * cian</u> maintained that he had <u>gra * sion * ed</u> the <u>shap * tion</u> only, and not his <u>shad * ow</u>. The traveler asserted that he had, with the hire of the <u>shap * tion</u>, hired his <u>shad * ow</u> also. The quarrel proceeded from words to <u>com * pli * ca * tions</u>, and while the men fought, the <u>shap * tion</u> galloped off.

In quarreling about the <u>shad * ow</u> we often lose the <u>sub * step * tion</u>.

Scoring: Number of underlined words correct   /25

Chap·ter 12
Final Assessment

Sequence	Suggested Time Frame	Moving to Automaticity	Time	Materials
Week 15: Final assessment	Day 1	Game—Final Bingo: Syllable Identification	20 min.	Final Bingo game board and word cards, playing pieces to cover spaces on cards, blank Bingo card
	Day 2	Game—Final Bingo: Syllable Identification from Day 1 cont'd.	20 min.	Final Bingo game board and word cards, playing pieces to cover spaces on cards, blank Bingo card
	Day 3	Game—Graduation	20 min.	Graduation game board and cards, playing pieces, die
	Day 4	Game—Graduation from Day 3 cont'd.	20 min.	Graduation game board and cards, playing pieces, die
	Days 1–5: Individual Assessments	Running Records	10 min.	Final assessment passage—student copy, Assessment matrix

Once you have completed the exercises in this book, the following activities will provide practice in using all the phonetic components. In the first review activity, students are asked to simply identify the type of syllable. In the second activity, they need to read the word and identify the syllable types.

The final assessment is an oral reading, which encompasses all the phonetic components covered in the book. This can be used diagnostically to determine student mastery.

Day 1

Game: Final Bingo—Syllable Identification

Chapter 12: Final Bingo game board
Chapter 12: Final Bingo word cards
Chapter 12: Blank Bingo card

Note: You can play this game on both Days 1 and 2.
- **Time:** Twenty minutes per day on two days.
- **Goal:** To identify the type of syllable in a dictated word.
- **Materials:** Final Bingo game board and word cards, playing pieces to cover spaces on cards, blank Bingo card.
- **Overview:** Groups of two to twenty students will identify syllable types in dictated words. The first student to cover a complete row is the winner.
- **Objective:** To be the first player to fill in five squares in a row by identifying the types of syllables in a dictated word.

Directions

1. Each player is given a blank Bingo card and completes her Bingo card by filling in the name of one of the six types of syllables in each box: CVC, CV, Cle, R-control, CVCe, and CVVC.

2. The word cards are shuffled and placed in a single pile.

3. The teacher reads the top word in the pile.

4. Players cover squares to match each of the types of syllables in the word. More than one square may be covered for each word. For example, given the word "table," players may cover squares for CV and Cle.

5. The first player to cover five boxes in a row vertically, horizontally, or diagonally is the winner.

6. The winner must have covered syllables that are contained in the words that were called.

7. If he makes a mistake, play continues until the next player has a complete row or column and can provide correct answer.

Day 2

Game: Final Bingo—Syllable Identification

Continue from Day 1.

Day 3

Game—Graduation

Chapter 12: Graduation game board
Chapter 12: Graduation game cards

Note: You can play this game on both Days 3 and 4.
- **Time:** Twenty minutes per day on two days.
- **Goal:** To read multisyllabic words and identify the types of syllables.
- **Materials:** Graduation game board and cards, playing pieces, die.
- **Objective:** To be the first player to reach home by reading multisyllabic words in isolation.
- **Overview:** Groups of two to seven students will read and identify the syllable types in words. The first student to reach home is the winner.

Directions

1. Dealer shuffles cards, deals five cards to each player, and places the remaining cards in a single pile in the center of the table.

2. Players roll a die. The player with the highest number will go first and play will continue around the table in a counterclockwise direction.

3. The first player rolls a die and moves that many spaces.

4. He reads the type of syllable on the space. If he has a card in his hand that has that type of a syllable in it, he reads the word.

5. If he reads the words correctly, he places the word face down on the bottom of the pile in the center of the table and his turn is complete.

6. If he reads the word incorrectly or does not have a card with that type of syllable on it, he picks up another card and places it in his hand, and then moves back to the square he was on before rolling the die.

7. If the player lands on a space with directions rather than a syllable type on it, he follows those directions rather than reading a card.

8. The first player to reach home is the winner.

Answers

ex * as * per * a * tion	CVC * CVC * R * CV * CVC
con * tem * pla * tion	CVC * CVC * CV * CVC
per * plex	R * CVC
con * spire	CVC * CVCe
re * fine	CV * CVCe
ho * ping	CV * CVC
tim * id	CVC * CVC
pu * pil	CV * CVC
ten * don	CVC * CVC
lav * ish	CVC * CVC
bus * tle	CVC * Cle
bri * dle	CV * Cle
brit * tle	CVC * Cle
cud * dle	CVC * Cle
rid	CVC
plume	CVCe
cane	CVCe
hope	CVCe
con * trive	CVC * CVCe
in * scribe	CVC * CVCe
con * sume	CVC * CVCe
de * fuse	CV * CVCe
pro * pose	CV * CVCe
de * cay	CV * CVVC or CV * CV
ap * peal	CV * CVVC
ab * stain	CVC * CVVC
vol * un * teer	CVC * CVC * CVVC
pre * vail	CV * CVVC
ail * ment	CVVC * CVC
en * gin * eer	CVC * CVC * CVVC
paup * er	CVVC * R
naut * ic * al	CVVC * CVC * CVC
aug * ment	CVVC * CVC
fraud * u * lent	CVVC * CV * CVC
toil * et	CVVC * CVC
loit * er * ing	CVVC * R * CVC
caus * tic	CVVC * CVC
al * loy	CVC * CVVC or CVC * CV
foy * er	CVVC * R or CV * R
ar * tic * u * late	R * CVC * CV * CVCe

Day 4

Game—Graduation

Continue from Day 3.

Days 1–5

Running Records

Chapter 12: Final assessment passage—student copy
Chapter 12: Assessment matrix

Running records are particularly helpful in identifying students' areas of need. This type of assessment is administered in a one-to-one setting. Two copies of the Final Assessment are included. The student is given the unmarked passage. The teacher circles the missed words on the underlined copy as the student orally reads the passage. Because this is a targeted reading assessment focusing on the syllables and phonetic patterns covered in this book, only the underlined words are evaluated.

After marking the words, the teacher will transfer the data to the assessment matrix. The words are listed on the matrix in the order they appear in the passage. For example, if the student missed the first underlined word "awakened," the teacher would circle the three "x's" in the columns after the word: CVC, CV, and Suffix. This procedure is repeated for each missed word. Add the number of circled "x's" in each column. Subtract that number from the total at the bottom of the column. This gives you the number correct in each category. Divide the number correct by the number of possible responses. This gives you a percentage of correct responses for each phonetic unit.

For example, if the teacher circled twelve "x's" in the CVC column, she would then subtract twelve from seventy-seven. The student would thus have sixty-five correct responses. Then the teacher would divide sixty-five by seventy-seven, which would be 84 percent. Using this procedure, the teacher is able to analyze the mastery of each phonetic component covered in *Teaching Syllable Patterns*. The teacher can then determine whether mastery has been achieved in each area or identify specific areas for reteaching.

Final assessment passage—student copy

Directions

Read the following passage orally to your teacher.

Early this morning I was awakened by an irritating, eardrum-breaking, relentless cacophony. Holding my pillow over my head didn't drown out the exasperating nuisance! I reluctantly got out of bed, staggered across the room and shut off the alarm. I was perplexed. It was 4:00 a.m.! It took only a minute for me to contemplate the situation and realize I shouldn't be feeling so annoyed and irritated. This was the most exciting day of my life!

I pulled back the window curtains and peered out, but wasn't surprised to find a somber, drizzle falling on the uninhabited street. A moment later, my father stumbled through my bedroom door and grumbled something about fifteen minutes. This was not an auspicious beginning to a momentous day. I wiggled into my jeans, grabbed my cellular phone, iPod, and luggage and stumbled down the stairs. The garage door was already ajar and the Lexus was in the drive with the trunk popped. I deposited my suitcase, a graduation present, in the trunk and hopped into the passenger side bucket seat.

Last spring I won a competitive internship for the summer with a House representative in Washington D.C., the federal capital. I submitted an essay, my high school transcripts, and three letters of recommendation from teachers and community members. Then in April I had a face-to-face interview and beat out 500 applicants for this esteemed position! Cool, huh?

I aspire to one day be a politician, so being offered this opportunity is going to be a stupendous experience. There is no debate. It will be sublime to achieve my dream.

Washington D.C.—what an astonishing place! I am really looking forward to exploring this historic city. I plan to peruse all the museums and stores. I have limited spending money, but I'm going to buy a copy of the Preamble of the Constitution to decorate my dorm room next year. Yes, I am a history geek.

My parental units were amazingly proud but understandably shocked when the information was delivered during the commencement ceremony.

In the autumn I am anticipating being a freshman at the University of Texas in Austin. I am hoping to major in government and history. Maybe one day, I will be a politician and some high school kid like me will be my enthusiastic intern.

Final assessment passage—teacher copy

Early this morning I was <u>awakened</u> by an <u>irritating</u>, <u>eardrum-breaking</u>, <u>relentless</u> <u>cacophony</u>. Holding my <u>pillow</u> over my head didn't <u>drown</u> out the <u>exasperating</u> <u>nuisance</u>! I <u>reluctantly</u> got out of bed, <u>staggered</u> <u>across</u> the room and shut off the <u>alarm</u>. I was <u>perplexed</u>. It was 4:00 a.m.! It took only a minute for me to <u>contemplate</u> the <u>situation</u> and <u>realize</u> I shouldn't be feeling so <u>annoyed</u> and <u>irritated</u>. This was the most <u>exciting</u> day of my life!

I pulled back the <u>window</u> <u>curtains</u> and <u>peered</u> out, but wasn't <u>surprised</u> to find a <u>somber</u>, <u>drizzle</u> falling on the <u>uninhabited</u> street. A <u>moment</u> later, my father <u>stumbled</u> through my bedroom door and <u>grumbled</u> something about <u>fifteen</u> minutes. This was not an <u>auspicious</u> beginning to a <u>momentous</u> day. I <u>wiggled</u> into my jeans, grabbed my <u>cellular</u> phone, ipod, and <u>luggage</u> and <u>stumbled</u> down the stairs. The <u>garage</u> door was already <u>ajar</u> and the Lexus was in the drive with the trunk <u>popped</u>. I <u>deposited</u> my <u>suitcase</u>, a <u>graduation</u> <u>present</u>, in the trunk and <u>hopped</u> into the <u>passenger side</u> <u>bucket</u> seat.

Last spring I won a <u>competitive</u> <u>internship</u> for the summer with a House <u>representative</u> in <u>Washington</u> D.C., the <u>federal</u> capital. I <u>submitted</u> an <u>essay</u>, my high school <u>transcripts</u>, and three letters of <u>recommendation</u> from teachers and <u>community</u> members. Then in April I had a face-to-face <u>interview</u> and beat out 500 <u>applicants</u> for this <u>esteemed</u> <u>position</u>! Cool, huh?

I <u>aspire</u> to one day be a <u>politician,</u> so being offered this <u>opportunity</u> is going to be a <u>stupendous</u> <u>experience</u>. There is no <u>debate</u>. It will be <u>sublime</u> to achieve my dream.

Washington D.C.—what an <u>astonishing</u> place! I am really looking <u>forward</u> to <u>exploring</u> this <u>historic</u> city. I plan to <u>peruse</u> all the museums and stores. I have limited spending money, but I'm going to buy a copy of the <u>Preamble</u> of the <u>Constitution</u> to <u>decorate</u> my dorm room next year. Yes, I am a history geek.

My <u>parental</u> units were <u>amazingly</u> <u>proud</u> but <u>understandably</u> shocked when the <u>information</u> was delivered during the <u>commencement</u> <u>ceremony</u>.

In the <u>autumn</u> I am <u>anticipating</u> being a freshman at the <u>University</u> of <u>Texas</u> in <u>Austin</u>. I am <u>hoping</u> to <u>major</u> in <u>government</u> and <u>history</u>. Maybe one day, I will be a <u>politician</u> and some high school kid like me will be my <u>enthusiastic</u> <u>intern</u>.

Readability—9.2 (Ninth grade, second month; if students are successfully reading this passage, they should be reading at or above grade level.)

Assessment matrix

Word	CVC	CV	Cle	R	CVCe	Suffix	CVVC	C/G	/Sh/
awakened	X	X				X			
irritating	X	X		X		X			
eardrum	X						X		
splitting	X					X			
relentless	X	X				X			
cacophony	X	X						X	
pillow	X						X		
drown							X		
exasperating	X	X		X		X			
nuisance						X	X		
reluctantly	X	X				X			
staggered	X			X		X			
across	X								
alarm	X			X					
perplexed	X			X		X			
contemplate	X				X			X	
situation	X	X							X
realize					X	X	X		
annoyed	X					X	X		
irritated	X	X		X		X			
exciting	X	X				X			
window	X						X		
curtains				X			X	X	
peered						X	X		
surprised				X		X			
somber	X			X					
drizzle	X		X						
uninhabited	X					X			
moment	X	X							
stumbled	X		X			X			
grumbled	X		X			X			
fifteen	X						X		
auspicious	X					X			X
momentous	X	X				X			
wiggled	X		X			X			
cellular	X	X						X	
luggage	X				X			X	
stumbled	X		X			X			
garage				X	X			X	
ajar	X			X					
popped	X					X			
deposited	X	X				X			
suitcase					X		X		
graduation	X	X							X
present	X								
hopped	X					X			
passenger	X							X	
bucket	X								
competitive	X					X		X	
internship	X			X		X			

Word	CVC	CV	Cle	R	CVCe	Suffix	CVVC	C/G	/Sh/
representative	X	X				X			
Washington	X								
federal	X			X					
submitted	X					X			
essay	X						X		
transcript	X								
recommendation	X	X							X
community	X	X						X	
interview	X			X			X		
applicants	X					X		X	
esteemed	X					X	X		
position	X	X							X
aspire	X				X				
politician	X								X
opportunity	X			X		X			
stupendous	X	X				X			
experience	X			X		X		X	
debate		X			X				
sublime	X				X				
astonishing	X					X			
forward				X					
exploring	X			X		X			
historic	X			X		X		X	
peruse				X	X				
Preamble	X	X	X						
Constitution	X	X							X
decorate	X			X	X				
parental	X			X		X			
amazingly	X	X				X			
proud							X		
understandably	X			X		X			
information	X	X		X					X
commencement	X					X		X	
ceremony	X	X		X		X		X	
autumn	X						X		
anticipating	X	X				X		X	
university	X	X		X		X			
Texas	X								
Austin	X						X		
hoping		X				X			
major		X		X					
government	X			X		X			
history	X			X					
politician	X					X		X	
enthusiastic	X	X				X		X	
intern	X			X					
	CVC	CV	Cle	R	CVCe	Suffix	CVVC	C/G	/Sh/
Total	**/81**	**/31**	**/6**	**/30**	**/8**	**/49**	**/17**	**/17**	**/8**

Ref·er·enc·es

Anderson, R. C., Hiebert, E. H., Scott, J. A., & Wilkinson, I. A. G. (1985). Becoming a Nation of Readers. Washington, D. C: The National Academy of Education & The Center for the Study of Reading.

Bhattarya, A. & Ehri, L. (2004). Graphosyllabic analysis helps adolescent struggling readers read and spell words. *Journal of Learning Disabilities*, 37, 331-348.

Curtis, M. E. (2004). Adolescents who struggle with word identification: research and practice. In T. L. Jetton & J. A. Dole (Eds.), *Adolescent literacy research and practice* (pp. 119-134). New York: The Guilford Press.

Kamil, M. (2003). *Adolescents and Literacy: Reading for the 21st century*. Washington, DC: Alliance for Excellent Education.

Moats. L. C. (2001). When older kids can't read. *Educational Leadership*, 58(6), 36-40.

National Institute of Child Health and Human Development (2004). Report of the National Reading Panel. Teaching children to read: An evidence-based assessment of the scientific research literature on reading and its implications for reading instruction. Retrieved May 10, 2008, from http://www.nationalreadingpanel.org.

National Institute for Literacy (2007). What content-area teachers should know about adolescent literacy. Retrieved May 10, 2008, from http://www.nifl.gov/nifl/Publications/adolescent_literacy07.pdf

Rippel, M. (2008). The six syllable types. Retrieved May 19, 2008, from http://www.bellaonline.com/articles/art36170.asp

Roswell, F., Chall, J., Curtis, M., & Kearns, G. (2005). *Diagnostic Assessments of Reading*. NJ: Riverside Publishing.

Smith, F. (1994). *Understanding Reading: A Psycholinguistic Analysis of Reading and Learning to Read*. Mahwah, NJ: Lawrence Erlbaum.

Torgesen, J.K. (2004). Lessons learned from the last 20 years of research on interventions for students who experience difficulty learning to read. In McCardle, P. & Chhabra, V. (EDS) *The voice of evidence in reading research*. Baltimore: Brookes Publishing.

Wilson, B. (1996). *Wilson Reading System Instructor Manual*. Oxford, MA: Wilson Language Training Corporation.

Woodcock, R. (1987). Woodcock Reading Mastery Tests Revised. Minneapolis: American Guidance Service, Inc.

CD Files

Chapter 2

CVC syllable prompts
Nonsense word list
Nonsense word prompts
Syllable combination prompts
Syllable chart
Blank Bingo card
Short vowel review worksheet
Post-test—CVC

Chapter 3

CV syllable chart
Syllable matching list
CV two-syllable word chart
Pot of Gold game board
Pot of Gold syllable cards
Open-syllable word search
Open-syllable crossword puzzle
Two-syllable word prompts
CV/CVC syllable word cards
Three-syllable word prompts
Post-test—CV

Chapter 4

Syllable matching list
Syllable sort graphic organizer
Syllable sort cards
Syllable fill-in-the-blanks
CV syllable prompts
Lists A and B
Medial syllables prompts
Syllable memory cards
CV/CVC worksheet
Nonsense word prompts
Post-test—CV and CVC

Chapter 5

Cle syllable graphic organizer
Cle syllable sort cards
ABC sort
Cle word chart

Cle fill-in-the-blanks
Baseball memory cards
Syllable chart
Cle word search
Post-test—Cle

Chapter 6

R-control vowel combination cards
R-control vowel word chart
R-control combination prompts #1
R-control combination prompts #2
Vocabulary graphic organizer
"Sportsmanship" story
Pyramid
R-control fill-in-the-blanks
R-control vowel worksheet #1
R-control vowel worksheet #2
Syllable matching list
Post-test—R-control syllables

Chapter 7

CVCe vocabulary fill-in-the-blanks #1
CVCe vocabulary fill-in-the-blanks #2
CVCe vocabulary fill-in-the-blanks #3
Rolling Along word cards
CVCe vocabulary fill-in-the-blanks #4
CVCe vocabulary fill-in-the-blanks #5
Cloze extension worksheet #1
CVCe vocabulary fill-in-the-blanks #6
CVCe vocabulary fill-in-the-blanks #7
Blend graphic organizer
Digraph graphic organizer
CVCe word list
Star-spangled cards
Star-spangled game board
CVCe vocabulary fill-in-the-blanks #8
Cloze extension worksheet #2
CVCe vocabulary fill-in-the-blanks #9
Multisyllabic CVCe word list
CVCe vocabulary fill-in-the-blanks #10
Post-test—CVCe

Chapter 8

Suffix fill-in-the-blanks #1
Suffix cards #1
Two-way suffix graphic organizer
Suffix fill-in-the-blanks #2
Root/suffix match #1
Category cards
Suffix cards #2
"Ing" cards
Root/suffix #2
Suffix worksheet
Root/suffix chart
Post-test—Suffixes

Chapter 9

Vowel combination prompts
Vowel team words
Homonym practice
Single-syllable vowel digraph cards
Multiple-syllable vowel digraph cards
Vowel combination word scramble
CVVC rhyme
Vowel team cards
Vowel team worksheet
Diphthong fill-in-the-blanks #1
Syllable matching #1
Diphthong cards
Word sort graphic organizer
Word sort list
Diphthong fill-in-the-blanks #2
Syllable matching #2
Racing Fever word cards
Racing Fever game board
Diphthong fill-in-the-blanks #3
Diphthong worksheet
Diphthong fill-in-the-blanks #4
Syllable prompts
"au/aw" cards
Syllable matching #3
Password set A cards
Password set B cards
Password help cards
Syllable matching #4
"aw/au" word search
Syllable count
Post-test—CVVC

Chapter 10

Soft "c" passage
"C" word sort graphic organizer #1
"C" word cards #1
Hard "c" passage
"C" word cards #2
"C" word sort graphic organizer #2
Checkers word board
"C" nonsense words
"C" worksheet
Soft "g" passage
"G" word sort graphic organizer #1
"G" word cards #1
Hard "g" passage
"G" word sort graphic organizer #2
"G" word cards #2
The Boss game board
The Boss cards
"G" nonsense words
"G" worksheet
Post-test—Soft and hard "C" and "G"

Chapter 11

/Sh/ passage #1
Root word prompts #1
/Sh/ word cards
Root word prompts #2
Target
Target word cards
Root word prompts #3
Root word prompts #4
Post-test—/Sh/

Chapter 12

Final Bingo game board
Final Bingo game cards
Blank Bingo card
Graduation game board
Graduation game cards
Final assessment passage—student copy
Assessment matrix